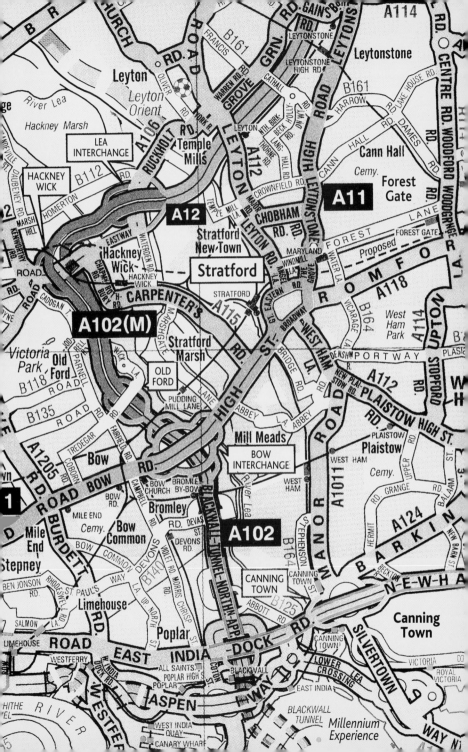

WHAT IF...?

With special thanks to all the contributors;

and to Faber & Faber, Macmillan and

Waterstones for all their good will and support

with cartoons by Steve Bell

Will Hutton

Bob Holman

Will Hobson

David Robinson

Andrew O'Hagan

Matthew Smerdon

Gordon Brown with Alya Din

Louise France

Stephen Jacobs

Jane Tewson

Daniel Silverstone

Steve Hilton

David Robinson

David Grayson

William Boyd

1 2 3 4 5 6 7 8 9 10 11 12 13 14 15

fifteen visions of change for Britain's inner cities

First published in 2000 by
The Short Book Company,
69/85 Tabernacle Street,
London EC2A 4RR

Copyright (C)
Community Links 2000

ISBN 0571 204376

Printed in Great Britain by
Hilo Colour Printers
Design: Georgia Vaux

Community Links is at
105 Barking Road,
London E16 4HQ
Tel: 0171 473 2270

ith cartoons by Steve Bell

'I want Leyton Orient Football Club to win the UEFA Champions League'

Bob, 37

INTRODUCTION

David Robinson

'Here is Edward Bear coming down the stairs now, bump bump bump on the back of his head. It is, as far as he knows, the only way of coming down the stairs but sometimes he feels there really is another way if only he could stop bumping for a moment and think of it.'

(Winnie-the-Pooh, A.A. Milne, 1926)

We marked our 21st anniversary at Community Links with an invitation to a selection of friends. An invitation for them to stop bumping for a moment, to step back from the daily routine and to consider their vision for our community. Everyone interpreted the brief in their own way. To some, 'community' meant Canning Town; to others, it meant the world. Each piece in this book stands alone as an independent perspective. Some contributors work for big organisations but they have all, myself included, written in a personal capacity.

The responses to our invitation have reminded me that Community Links' friends are a varied bunch – they don't agree about everything. But they are also constructive and visionary, just as our founding Trustees were 21 years ago. At that time we had more beliefs than belongings. When we moved into our first permanent home – a tiny lock-up shop in East Ham – we had a Calor gas-fire, enough rent for six weeks and a clear mission: 'We all,' I wrote at the time, 'need help at some time in our lives, we all have something to contribute. Community Links will work on developing practical new ways of tackling our local problems and will involve the whole community in the process.'

The gas-fires were scrapped years ago and we have moved headquarters three times, but the same principles still underpin all that we do. Last year more than 25,000 people benefited from Community Links projects, run by more than 450 volunteers in 60 key sites. Crucially, 80 per cent of our frontline services were delivered by people who had first become involved as users of those services. Our mission statement spells out the approach:

'To generate change. To tackle causes not symptoms, find solutions not palliatives. To recognise that we all need to give, as well as to receive and to appreciate that those who experience a problem understand it best. To act local but think global, to teach but never stop learning. To distinguish between the diversity that enriches our society and the inequalities that diminish it. To grow – but all to build a network not an empire. To be driven by dreams, judged on delivery. To never do things for people but to guide and support, to train and enable, to simply inspire.'

We no longer believe, as perhaps we once did, that Community Links will change the world. But over the last 21 years, hundreds and hundreds of individual worlds have been shaped and, day in day out, are being shaped, if not by us then with us. First, we offer support in times of crisis; then the opportunity to participate – in playgroups, supplementary education, training courses, counselling groups, advice services, and so on – and to discover, alongside others, the power within. One of the first 12-year-olds to drop into our little East Ham shop all those years ago is now a full-time worker on our detached youth-work team; and one of the early graduates from our Education programme has grown up to manage our Holiday programme – the biggest of its kind in the country. No flashes and bangs but steady support, determined belief, growth, fulfilment.

Beyond these personal achievements, we recognise the scale of the challenge: one in four households here in Newham lives on or below the official poverty line. Across the UK, 14 million people manage on an annual income that is less than half the national average, and beyond these shores one in five live and die in poverty.

Some can read these figures and say, 'I can't possibly make a difference to that.' But when we listen to some of the 4,000 people who use our Canning Town centre every week, *we* believe: 'We *did* make a difference for Mustapha, we *did* make a difference for Janice...'

At the start of the new Millennium, it is time for us to reflect on our place in the world and our moment in history. We are of the generation that has wired the world. We *can* make a difference – individually and collectively. We have the technology and the wealth to include the excluded, here and across the globe. Have we the will?

This is no book of dreams. If some contributors build castles in the air, their foundations are in Canning Town. As Community Links comes of age we offer this compilation to celebrate, to share ideas we believe in and, above all, to *simply inspire*.

David Robinson is the director of Community Links

'Politicians need to be honest about what the *real* issues are. It's not just about poster campaigns'

Brian, 71

Number 1

The Economics of Poverty

WILL HUTTON

Twenty years ago the argument for redistribution was too little challenged. Now it is too little made

Britain today boasts nearly 50,000 millionaires, and record levels of income inequality. Million-pound houses are not yet commonplace, but they will start to be within two or three years. Over the 1980s and 1990s, as income inequality in this country has reached American levels – the top 10 per cent of the working population in Britain now earns the equivalent of the bottom 50 per cent – so we are developing an American structure of house prices and neighbourhoods. Upmarket districts all over Britain, not only in the privileged parts of London where ordinary people could once expect to be able to buy a house, have become exclusive enclaves, mirroring the 40,000 or so 'drawbridge communities' in the US. Their occupants do not yet live behind steep fences and security cameras, though that is happening in some of the newer developments, but the invisible wall is real none-the-less.

It's a situation which can only get worse. As house-price inflation in favoured districts reaches astronomic proportions, economics is reinforcing ancient prejudices. The stock of homes in so-called 'good' locations is finite – there is only one Hampstead, only one North Oxford; at the same time, the volume of cash chasing these luxury enclaves is growing exponentially, driven by today's staggering salaries. The new super-rich, able to support mortgages of half a million pounds or more, buy into the rich neighbourhoods, leaving those on the outside with a choice: either they stay where they are, within affordable limits, in poor and middle-income neighbourhoods, and soon find themselves priced out of the higher property bracket; or they take the risk of borrowing to the hilt to buy into the rich neighbourhood as quickly as possible to ride the boom – and so increase the demand.

The results of this property chase are pernicious, and undermine every institution in which some notion of equal access or equal opportunity is important. The first casualty is education: comprehensive schools become the prisoners of their catchment areas. The comprehensives rising up the league tables are those in middle-class areas; those failing are the ones locked in areas of poverty, where there is zero chance of relief. Children from un-stable or broken homes, where the parents are at their wits' end from lack of money, necessarily have lower expectations of themselves and perform less well at school than children from richer homes. Comprehensive education becomes a mockery.

So does good health. The poor are more at risk from heart disease, lung cancer and obesity, and as the poor tend to become ever more concentrated in disadvantaged areas, so all the factors which contribute to poor health are reinforced. For example, shops selling fresh vegetables, fruit, meat and fish – items which are more expensive than mass-produced tinned and processed food – tend not to prosper. So eating well, even if families have the income, becomes much more difficult. Drug use is pervasive, and drugs – or at least the need to find the cash to buy drugs – bring with them an increase in petty crime, and sometimes not so petty crime. It is this cycle of reinforcing adverse trends which causes the deprivation that blights both the inner city and the outlying social housing estates.

Here, too, is the incubation process that creates the giant pools of largely unemployable men; the young in poor neighbourhoods become isolated, dissociated from the wider community, while middle-aged men are locked out of the labour market through a lack of skills and/or opportunity. Even after five years of economic growth averaging at about three per cent and a fall in unem-ployment to 1.3 million, some 2.5 million people over 50 (but still of working age) in Britain sit idle or are economically inactive. A fifth of British households have nobody at work; in the river valleys of the old industrial conurbations like Strathclyde, Merseyside and Tyneside this proportion rises to 30 per cent.

And so Britain's great industrial cities are declining. With their

Inequality not only divides our cities,

inhabitants migrating to the suburbs or towards London and the South East, their populations have shrunk by more than 500,000 over the last 20 years; and the rate of loss is accelerating. Those who move away leave behind urban areas desolated by neglect and poverty. The argument that unemployment is soluble only by 'flexible labour markets', in which the unemployed price themselves into work by accepting lower wages, is at best a partial view of the solution and at worst callous and uncomprehending. The reality is that unemployment is a feature of geography. To invite Liverpool, Bradford or Sunderland to 'price themselves' into work is self-defeating. There is no work for these cities to price themselves into. Their entire urban fabric is decaying; demand is low; business is poor; the public sector is in retreat. They are locked into low wages, reducing demand and yet more decline.

Should we care? For those at the receiving end of this process the reasons for concern are obvious, but why should the rest of society give a damn? In vain do economists and some politicians argue that inequality carries its own costs – in lost taxes, lost

so pollutes our minds and sensibilities

workers, lost lives and burgeoning public expenditure. For those enjoying the benefits of the house-price boom, executive share-options or once unaffordable luxuries this argument cuts little ice. They are all right, thank you.

The proper answer is that they are not all right. They may be enjoying high house prices, but only by requiring the next generation to borrow to the hilt to support them – and the next generation is their children. But there is a more subtle argument still. As Plato argued, there can be no friendship among unequals. Inequality not only divides our cities and undermines our neighbourhoods, it also, as the South Africans discovered with apartheid, colonises and pollutes our minds and sensibilities. We become coarsened by our growing inability to empathise with the circumstances and conditions of our poorer neighbours.

Social exchange is based on reciprocity; once the gulf grows too large between the rich and the poor, or even between the middle-income groups and the poor, there is no basis for reciprocity. An unequal society shrinks the space in which human beings can interact and reciprocate each others' actions; the language and moral codes which underpin our collective consciousness balkanise and fragment. At the bottom of the pile, an opted-out underclass – as much as 10 per cent of the adult population – constructs its own culture, in which crime is seen as a legitimate source of income and work comes to be regarded as barely worthwhile; at the top, members of an opted-out superclass buy their own private education, health and transport and see no reason to share in the commonweal. As far as they are concerned, taxation is an insupportable burden and the public sector a second-class provider of last resort.

This social fragmentation is not a source of individual happiness for either the rich or the poor. The rich get locked in a lonely world of competitive consumption in which material acquisitions gradually replace human association. Nobody enjoys living in a city or urban space in which there are increasingly no-go areas. For the poor, there is not only the desolation of poverty, but the growing awareness that the capacity to close the gap between themselves and even those on average incomes is impossible. Living with inequality is not just morally insupportable; it cuts us all off from the well-springs of our own humanity.

What to do? First, a humanitarian concern about the *fact* of inequality – rather than just the problems it causes – must enter the national debate. This will require politicians of the Left to give a lead. There is always a tension in a democracy between those who argue for liberty and freedom, and those who argue for equality and public action to assert these values. It is true that a *wholly* equal society is a pipe-dream – only enforceable by a degree of social control and income redistribution that even most of those on the Left would now regard as anathema; but a wholly free society, in which any social outcome is permissible, would be no less realistic or tolerable. The real argument is about degree. Twenty years ago the arguments for redistribution were too little challenged; now the argument for redistribution is too little made, and the pendulum has swung too far towards the Right.

New Labour, in this respect, is part of the problem rather than the solution. Although it has launched some innovative social programmes, and covertly found the resources from the rich, it has refused to explain that its objective is the reduction of inequality. Redistribution is the noun that dare not speak its name. For example, in its 1999 Poverty Audit, the Government committed itself to a list of measures aimed at combating poverty, but nowhere among these was there actually a target for narrowing the income gap to bring the living standards of the poor nearer to the average. Tony Blair, in his speech to the 1999 Labour Party conference, conspicuously committed himself to creating equality of *worth*; tackling equality of *outcome*, though, is still off the agenda.

If there is no political narrative in which to locate the sort of individual policies that will really address poverty, the pass is sold. So, although the Government's policy initiatives together represent a marked change of direction from the Conservatives, they have made little impact on the national debate. The combined effect of Sure Start (its programme for the under-threes), the Working Family Tax Credit, the New Deal and the targeted increases in welfare benefits, especially for children, will be significantly to reduce the poverty of families and children. But this is the social democratic programme that must stay in the closet. For New Labour is reluctant to argue that social deprivation or educational disadvantage are linked to poverty; rather, they are linked to weak work incentives or badly run schools. Socio-economic conditions, the Government argues, are no excuse for poor performance, or indeed any explanation of it – a denial of reality which does it no credit, even if it is true that work incentives could be enhanced and schools better managed.

And nor, for much the same reasons, does New Labour want to argue that the rich have quite as many obligations as the poor. The Government's aim is to pull the jobless into the world of work, without reforming either the distribution of national income or the wider culture of the rich. Nothing must disturb Middle England.

Yet if the Left do not make this case, nobody else will. In the absence of any rallying call to reduce inequality, the political debate is becoming increasingly dominated by rival bids to lower taxes and roll back the state. There are limits to how far a political party can act Left while talking Right; ultimately the legitimacy of its action hangs on winning the argument and assembling a coalition to back it. New Labour is winning no arguments over inequality, nor assembling any coalition that might do anything about it. And without this sort of initiative, whole areas of policy are being left unexplored and undebated.

I would argue that, if we are to make any real impact on the inequality in Britain in the new Millennium, there are six key areas which need to be examined:

1. Taxation

Any programme to lower inequality must surely address the incomes and privileges of the rich. The marginal rates of both income tax and inheritance tax should be higher; everybody knows it, especially the rich. Property taxes are too low, and there should be a higher rate of VAT for luxuries, so that higher-value goods bought by the rich provide proportionally more tax. The upper earnings limit for National Insurance contributions should also be removed. At least £5 billion of extra tax could be paid each year by the rich.

2. Income at the top

The system for determining executive pay needs to be wholly overhauled; at the moment it is a case of 'You-scratch-my-back-and-I'll-scratch-yours'. British company law allows board members complete discretion over whom they appoint to the remuneration committees that determine both their salaries and share-options and those of senior management. The system should be opened up. Remuneration committees ought to be staffed by a majority of independent directors, and their recommendations made public and voted on by share-holders.

3. Income at the bottom

There needs to be a big boost to the incomes of the poor. British Income Support is extraordinarily mean – it is scarcely possible to live on what is paid to men and women out of work today. The basic presumption of social insurance should be restored; everyone pays in and everyone should get a liveable income out – though, of course, this entitlement should not be unqualified; there should be a reciprocal obligation on the part of the person receiving benefits to look for work after a certain period. The old-age pension should be restored as the basic building block in retirement – at present it is simply being allowed to wither on the vine. And so-called private or stakeholder pensions based on individual savings in the stock-market should be treated with caution; they automatically favour the rich who can make larger contributions, and they are in any case extremely vulnerable to changes in stock-market fortunes. There should be a massive investment in improving public health facilities in poorer areas.

4. Education

Improving the standards of 5- to 11-year-olds in primary schools is crucial. The aim should be for 100 per cent of 11-year-olds to reach the basic literacy standards, not merely 80 per cent – this would bring vital educational returns as the children move up through the system. At a rough estimate it would cost about £2 billion a year to halve current state class sizes – and so bring them in line with those in the private sector. This, too, would yield the highest possible social returns; and, with public finances moving into a structural surplus of more than one per cent of GDP rising, the Government can no longer argue that such a programme is too expensive. Lowering secondary school class sizes, improving teacher training and teachers' pay could follow. In the meantime, the charitable status of private schools should be withdrawn, or at least made conditional on them opening their doors to more pupils from poorer homes. Selection procedures for university should be biased in favour of poorer kids in order to redress some of the advantage conferred by birth into richer homes.

5. Inner-city regeneration

We need to make an innovative attempt to reinvent our cities, especially in the North. The recommendations made by the Urban Task Force, chaired by Lord Rogers, are a useful beginning: cheap public transport; housing designed for users who do not drive cars; effective land taxation; devolving planning to local communities, and so on.

6. Employment

The core issue, though, in any programme to tackle deprivation, is employment. Here the entire support structure of the business world needs to be re-examined. British companies, trying to maximise 'shareholder value', are becoming more and more demanding as employers, insisting on short-term contracts, longer hours and lower pay. British company law, the structure of the financial system which demands high rates of return as the *quid pro quo* for investment, the management culture of British business… all these things require an overhaul if Britain is to move towards a 'knowledge economy' with higher paid and more secure jobs.

And so the list goes on. Some policies will be more effective than others; some will need more consideration to be got right. But there is no point in even opening up a debate on the subject until there is a more widespread recognition that inequality is high and rising, and that this is doing none of us any good. We do not have to be hair-shirt egalitarians to make the case for lower inequality, nor to live like saints as exemplars of our philosophy. We simply need to protest about what is currently happening and argue for better. That at least would be a beginning.

Will Hutton is a contributing editor to the *Observer* and chief executive of the Industrial Society. His book, *The State We're In*, is available in paperback (Vintage, £7.99)

'It doesn't make sense: sometimes they pull buildings down and then don't do anything with the space, and sometimes they build on the parks. I'd like them to make a park where there isn't any broken glass and that you don't have to go under the motorway to get to'

Stacey, 14

BOB HOLMAN

Number 2

A Vision from Easterhouse

The new Millennium offers all of us an opportunity to redress the imbalance that exists in British society: to show a bias *towards* the poor

The invitation to write this piece reached our flat in Glasgow in June 1999. As I read the news of the month, I perceived much of what I dislike about Britain. The media was full of the wedding of Edward Windsor and Sophie Rhys-Jones. It was announced that they had been given the titles, 'Their Royal Highnesses The Earl and Countess of Wessex'. Why? This couple appear to have no outstanding abilities. They were not elected. The explanation is that they are who they are by an accident of birth. Edward has inherited titles and power. Such a situation is an affront to democracy.

In times gone by, Labour leaders like Keir Hardie and George Lansbury spoke out passionately against an hereditary monarchy. Today New Labour ministers are as infatuated with royalty as the Conservatives are. In June, the Government gave a clear signal of its support for the House of Lords: Tony Blair dished out titles to a number of his followers. New Labour may have made a commitment to reforming the hereditary principle in the Lords, but it does not appear to feel any need to ensure that the members of the upper house are democratically elected. As things stand, those members will continue to owe their positions to patronage; they will also presumably be happy to continue having public money spent on maintaining the comfort of their surroundings in the upper house and on keeping up their excessive attendance allowances.

Other news items in June illustrated the vast inequalities that exist in this country. Elton John was shown to possess a fortune of £160 million and to have spent £250,000 a week with credit cards. Jack Cunningham, the former Minister for the Cabinet Office, so shocked civil servants with his extravagance while on official business that one of them leaked details of his stay in a £1,000-a-night hotel along with a visit to a game reserve. Tony Blair was preparing to take his family for another holiday in a luxury villa in Italy. New Labour advisors received substantial hikes in their salaries – one worth £4,000 a year. In the same month, I had to help a working mother with a large family who had turned to a loan shark to buy household goods. Her wage is £123 a week. I purchased trainers for some kids who had no shoes. I read that 35 per cent of British households cannot afford a holiday away from home.

On 14 June the *Daily Mail* published an article by the Prime Minister in which he condemned young single mothers as a threat to family life and as a drain on the public purse. Noticeably, he does not condemn the morals of tax evasion by the wealthy. The poor are despised in Britain. To its credit, the Government has established a Social Exclusion Unit. But excluded from the Unit's 12 members is anyone on a low income. In June, I also watched *Question Time* on BBC television. All the panel members came from the privileged and powerful classes. There is a bias against the poor. They are excluded from any control over and participation in the decisions that shape their lives. When you consider this in conjunction with the huge material inequalities that they are faced with, it is surely no surprise to learn that, according to the Government's Urban Task Force (chaired by Lord Rogers), British cities have the deepest social divisions in western Europe. A divided society.

Britain is marred by a lack of democracy, by the oppression of poor people. So what? My objections spring from my Christian socialism. I believe God created all people of equal value: it follows that all people should be given the opportunity to contribute to the shape of our society and, in particular, that anyone who holds a position of power, responsibility or privilege should be elected to that position. I believe God made all people of equal worth: it follows that the resources of the earth should be distributed as equally as possible. I am sure that God, in the person of Christ, displayed a particular concern for the poor. And I see democratic socialism as the political means most likely to build a society consistent with these beliefs.

At present, Britain contains two, very different kinds of estates. There are the estates of royalty, the Lords and politicians, all of which are sustained by a seemingly limitless flow of wealth; and then there are the other ones. In Easterhouse, in Glasgow, where I work, more than 80 per cent of the school children qualify for clothing grants – that is, they come from families with very low incomes. This is an estate which is in dire need of any wealth it can get its hands on.

What it does have, though, is a fair number of small neighbourhood groups, set up by the inhabitants themselves to help meet the needs of their own community – and it is these which I have put at the heart of my vision for the Millennium. One of the groups, FARE (Family Action in Rogerfield & Easterhouse), is based in five flats that became hard-to-lets following drug deaths within them. FARE runs activities for more than 300 children a week, a breakfast club, a café, education classes for adults and so on.

In June, I attended its monthly management committee, the members of which are elected by residents. We discussed the forthcoming holidays for 100 children: grants had been obtained to subsidise them. We regretted that FARE could no longer afford and in fact had had to sell its caravan, which for years had provided cheap holidays for families. And so back to the perennial subject of finance.

FARE has six excellent staff – including two lone parents who can work because the project is on their doorstep. The group receives no money from local or central government to help pay its staff's low salaries, and could not survive without the backing of sympathetic charitable trusts. The committee members are local people who receive no payments and will never get establishment gongs. They come because they are committed to their community and because they have a bias towards the poor. I have found something very precious among the committee, the staff and users of FARE. Theirs is a fellowship derived from acting together for the well-being of others.

My vision for Millennium Britain is threefold:

■ I want a more *democratic* society. I hope that the monarchy is abolished in the early years of the Millennium. A Christian opposed to the royal family? Of course. The Bible reveals a God who reluctantly allowed his people to have kings. Later they were removed because of their arrogance and their disregard for the oppressed. If the British royals were sent packing, then the hereditary principle would be undermined, the principle of democracy would be strengthened, and the royal family's huge wealth could be redistributed among the poor.

■ I want a Britain *without* the House of Lords. If a second chamber is required then it ought to be an elected body. Not least, the abolition of appointed peers would end the sycophancy towards the establishment displayed by those who covet the glory of ermine and titles.

■ I want a more *equal* society. I won't live to see it but I long for a Britain in which the current huge and brutal material differences are reduced. I propose the introduction of a maximum income, so that no one will be able to earn more than three times what anyone else earns. I look forward to a society in which all are in decent homes, in which all children are properly fed. A society in which all families will be able to afford recreation without recourse to charitable subsidies – not one in which the privileged few own holiday homes, enjoy leisure on their own boats and pilot planes for pleasure. Greater equality, far from making people into uniform robots, will release the creative abilities of millions of socially deprived citizens. As people draw closer together in terms of incomes and possessions, so they will draw closer together in fellowship. A more united, less divisive Britain.

Above all, then, I want a more *participative* Britain. OK, I dream. But this is a piece about a vision. In reality, I recognise that there is not any immediate prospect of a more democratic and equal society. New Labour is taking us into the new Millennium and it will do nothing to offend royalty; it is opposed to making even the fat cats – those with annual incomes of more than £70,000 – pay more income tax.

That said, the governments of the early years of the new era might allow a more participative society. FARE is only one example of a neighbourhood group. There are thousands of other small, struggling projects. Participation is the key word. It means that the project staff are locals, who live in the area, rather than professionals who commute in and out of it. It means these staff can make a long-term commitment, not simply put in a three-year stint. It means, too, the promotion of values and practices involving altruism, service and collectivity. It often results in disadvantaged individuals becoming stronger people as they contribute to their neighbourhood.

The trouble is that neighbourhood groups are largely unrecognised and under-financed. Last year saw the establishment of the Millennium Promise Fund, an initiative organised by business firms, under which employees throughout the country were encouraged to donate the earnings of their last hour's work in 1999. However, none of the proceeds of this fund is due to go directly to neighbourhood groups; instead, the financial flow will be towards the national, multimillion-pound voluntary bodies (bodies like Barnardo's, which already has an annual income of £109 million and net assets of £196 million). Why does central government refuse to finance independent local projects run by poor people?

In order to facilitate a more participative Millennium, my proposal is that the Government should establish and finance a National Neighbourhood Fund. The Fund would allocate cash to Neighbourhood Trusts, which would give grants to existing and new locally controlled neighbourhood groups in deprived areas. Residents from these areas would elect members of the Trusts. The Trusts in their turn would elect members of the Fund committee. The outcomes would be as follows:

■ Greater participation among the residents of deprived areas in neighbourhood groups as existing ones expand and new ones are started.

■ More power to low-incomed citizens as they become involved in bodies which decide who and what should receive grants.

■ Better services as groups receive stable funding.

■ More jobs in places of high unemployment as neighbourhood groups take on more local staff.

Politics is not just about government. Whatever governments decide about greater democracy, equality and participation in the New Millennium, we as individuals can live the kinds of lives which support these ends.

First, we can refuse to take incomes which are above the national average. In short, we can reject inequality.

Second, we can decline to seek advancement or honours by

currying favour with the political, lordly or royal establishments. In short, we can reject patronage, which is the foe of democracy.

Third, we can dwell alongside citizens who are in the greatest social need: send our children to their schools, use their shops, identify with their neighbourhood groups, and enjoy their fellowship. In short, we can display a bias towards the poor.

This collective action with poor people must not be done in a patronising or controlling manner. Such impositions are likely to offend residents and to decrease their participation. Rather it has to be done gradually and with a commitment to staying. The approach is best summed up in what Jesus Christ called 'servanthood'. If many more individuals adopted these attitudes and practices then they might become a movement which would challenge the prevailing vices of selfishness, greed and arrogance. If the movement became widespread, then even the Government would have to take note.

The case for living according to principles does not win political or media attention. Politicians like Lord Hattersley write reams about the virtues of equality but not a word about how their beliefs affect their own personal behaviour. Indeed, Hattersley, when an MP, was revealed to be top of the pile in terms of his outside earnings – which amounted to £104,300, in addition to his pay and expenses as an MP. Champagne socialists sometimes justify their hypocrisy on the grounds that individual actions cannot alter social malaises. I find this an illogical cop-out. The implication is that, while believing in greater equality, we can still take huge incomes, accumulate possessions and distance ourselves from poor people and so adopt all the practices which reinforce inequality. If I am opposed to the taking of hard drugs, it is not sufficient to write articles suggesting national policies to counter them – I must refrain from taking drugs myself. In like manner, if we desire a society based on equality, democracy and the end of social divisions then we must live lives which express these values. Unless individuals live differently, the new Millennium will be no better than the old.

Bob Holman is a Visiting Professor in the Social Policy department at Glasgow University, and is a voluntary neighbourhood worker in Easterhouse. He writes, with Carol, Bill, Erica, Anita, Denise, Penny and Cynthia, in *Faith in the Poor* (Lion Publishing, £7.99)

2

'Children should be able to go out without their parents being scared about what might happen to them'

Jagadish, 11

Number 3

The London Borough of Newham in Facts and Stats

WILL HOBSON

When reduced to a list of facts and statistics, the London Borough of Newham emerges as anything but average or ordinary

Population in 1997: 228,500 (the 'unofficial' population, however, is known to be much higher)

Newham has the highest birth-rate in London. (In 1997 the average birth-rate was 20.2 births per 1,000 residents, compared to 14.8 births per 1,000 in London as a whole)

1 in 3 households have an income of less than £141 a week (compared to 1 in 8 households in England and Wales)

Percentage of households earning £640 per week, or over: 7% (the smallest percentage in London)

The unemployment rate is more than twice the national average of 5.2%

A quarter of people of working age are long-term unemployed, ie for more than a year

Chances that someone under 25 is unemployed: 1 in 4

Percentage of local firms which employ between 1 and 10 employees: 81%

Percentage of firms which employ more than 200 employees: 1%

In March 1998, 10,897 people were unemployed and only 360 new

Will Hobson Facts and Stats

vacancies were advertised in the Job Centres

1 in 5 people aged 16 or over are claiming Income Support. (Between the mid-1980s and mid-1990s, the number of people on Income Support increased by 93%)

Chances that a resident is under 15 years old: 1 in 4

Percentage of children who live in households with no wage earner: 35.2% (compared to 20.2% of children in London as a whole)

Percentage of households in which children are brought up by single parents: 10.5% (compared to a London average of 7.5%)

Percentage of first-time visitors to Community Links who are not claiming all the benefits they're entitled to: 50%

42% of primary school pupils and 44% of secondary school pupils are eligible for free school meals

Only half of secondary school pupils who are eligible for free school meals actually take advantage of them

Percentage of households with no car: 51.4% (compared to a national average of 30%)

Percentage of the weekly Job-seekers' Allowance that one would need to spend to buy a weekly bus pass: 24%

Food shopping in local shops costs on average 46% more than in a large superstore, yet the majority of people live at least

3

one bus ride away from the larger stores

Number of restaurants in the borough run by Idi Amin's fifth wife, Sarah K Amin: 1. (The S Restaurant in Upton Lane – at their wedding in Kampala in 1975 Yasser Arafat was the best man and the food alone was reputed to cost £2 million)

Percentage of residents who are owner-occupiers: 49.8% (compared to 57.2% in London as a whole)

It is still the cheapest borough for house prices in London. The average price for a property in Newham is £63,700, compared to a current average price of £140,000 for London as a whole. (But since its two-up-two-downs are among the few central London properties within the range of the average first-time buyer, and since it is close to the new Jubilee Line extension, parts of the borough – especially 'Stratford Village' – are undergoing a mini-boom. A two-bedroom terraced house in Tennyson Road, E15, cost £52,000 in 1996, £65,000 in January 1999 and £80,000 in July 1999)

Percentage of private houses which are deemed unfit for human habitation:15%

Number of families in the borough who are living in temporary accommodation: 2,100

East London boroughs have an estimated 20-40,000 homeless people

The three most overcrowded local authorities in England are all in East London – Tower Hamlets, Newham and Hackney

Percentage of residents who rent from the local authority: 30.76% (compared to 23.3% of residents in London as a whole)

Percentage of council tenants who are more than 13 weeks behind on their rent: 11.7%

Amount of Council Tax presently uncollected: £4.9 million

Number of summonses issued by the Council during the three years of the Poll Tax: 170,127; number of cases in which bailiffs were instructed: 57,041; number of arrest warrants issued: 2,259

Percentage of households which claim housing benefit: 40%

More than 1 in 5 households have no central heating

If half of all the households in the borough took up composting, 8,000 tonnes of waste would be diverted from landfill sites

Pensioners make up a smaller proportion of Newham's population than the London average but they are more likely:
a) to be suffering from long-term debilitating illnesses (43% as opposed to 39.2% London-wide)
b) not to have central heating (35.7% as opposed to 30.3% London-wide)
c) either not to have a bathroom/shower, or inside WC, or to have to share one with someone else (12% as opposed to 4.2% London-wide)

Just under half of the population come from an ethnic minority group (compared to an average ethnic minority population London-wide of 24%)

Percentage of people moving into the borough in 1991 who were first-time migrants from overseas: 64% (compared to an average of 34% of people in other London boroughs)

Unemployment rate among the borough's ethnic minority groups: 30.1%

Number of languages used by callers to the East London and City Health Authority's language line in an average year: 37

Percentage of language needs which were met by advice and interpretation services in hospitals and primary healthcare services in East London: 35%

The mortality rate in the borough is 14% higher and the illness rate 27% higher than the national average

Rate at which people under 65 die from coronary heart disease: 59.1 per 1,000 (compared to 42 per 1,000 for England and Wales as a whole)

Percentage of mothers who make contact with health services in the first three months of pregnancy: 10%

7.5 children per every 1,000 live births die under the age of 1 (compared to 6.1 in England and Wales as a whole)

Chances that a child will be registered with one of the borough's 79 dental practices: 1 in 3

Newham has the highest rate of tuberculosis in England, and it is rising

Percentage of hospital in-patient stays attributable to mental disorders: 28%

Number of times, per head, the East London and City Health Authority prescribed medicine in 1997: 10.7 (compared to 8.7 per head in London as a whole)

In 1998 a Newham GP, Dr. Prasanta Bhowmik, was the first GP to receive the BMA's Sir James Cameron Award

Number of head-teachers in the borough's 87 schools replaced in the last six years: 20

Chances that a member of the teaching staff has been replaced in the last three years: 1 in 3

Although Newham, Hackney and Tower Hamlets took three of the bottom four places of 125 English education authorities in 1998, Newham is the borough which has shown the most improvement. In 1997, for the first time, more than a third of pupils gained five grade A to C passes at GCSE, as they did in 1998 – a 45% improvement on 1994. Moreover, only 3.2% leave school with no qualifications (compared to 6.6% nationally)

It has the highest number of per capita nursery education places in London: 4,488

It has the second lowest pupil exclusion rate in London. In 1997-98, 54 children (0.12% of the total pupil population) were permanently excluded from their schools

Three years ago, its pupil attendance rates were the sixth worst in the country; now they are running at an average of 90%, the fourth best of all inner London authorities

Percentage of population with a higher education qualification: 9% (compared to 18% in London as a whole)

Crime in 1997/8 was 16% above the average for the Metropolitan Police District

Criminal damage and violence against a person occurred 28% more than the Metropolitan Police District average, and there was a 71% higher rate of robbery

Number of cases of residential burglary in 1997/8: 1,722

Number of CCTV cameras used to survey the performance of council dustmen: 159

Newham has the highest insurance premiums in England

In 1996/7 the parking department at Newham council made a net loss; in the same year, Westminster City council's parking department made a profit of £32.7 million

Number of hectares of urban parks and open spaces in the borough: 151

Number of hectares of derelict land – land which is so damaged by industrial or other development that it cannot be converted to beneficial use without treatment: 243

The Three Mills Heritage Centre, a group of 18th-century buildings on the River Lea, contains Europe's largest tidal mill

Number of Vietnam war films shot on location in Newham: 1

Will Hobson is a freelance journalist and researcher; his column, Hobson's Choice, appears in the *Independent on Sunday*

'You hear people talking about social exclusion but there are still people sitting outside this category, refugees for example. We need to target those who don't even get included in the thinking about the "poverty line". To do so, we need community-relevant, flexible and risk-friendly strategies'

Michael, 29

Number 4

Accounting for the Uncounted

DAVID ROBINSON

Until we account for the Uncounted – people who, for whatever reason, are transient and 'off-register' – we will continue to underestimate the real scale of need in Britain's most deprived areas

In recent years we have become increasingly aware of the growing number of Community Links users who are permanent East London residents, but who are not registered as living here. Our experience suggests that this Uncounted population is largely made up of refugees, asylum-seekers, travellers and others – mainly 16- to 24-year-olds – who are, for whatever reason, transient and 'off register', as well as significant numbers of the very poorest people who disappeared when the Poll Tax was introduced in 1988. Almost certainly, some are here illegally or want to preserve their anonymity for particular reasons. Most, however, have nothing to hide and haven't consciously hidden. They are simply outside and unable to find a way in.

We believe that the East London population is not only significantly bigger than the census figure for the area, but also that the deprivation in it is more extreme and the exclusion more acute than anything suggested in the official statistics, which reveal extraordinary inconsistencies. Consider, for instance, the experience of the East London and City Health Authority (ELCHA). The total official population in the area is between 605,000 and 610,000. But GP registrations number 710,000, and ELCHA believes that it serves an actual resident patient population of between 635,000 and 650,000.

The problem is that the sorts of people that we identify as Uncounted are also those who are most likely to gather in the poorest areas. As Newham and Hackney are two of the most deprived boroughs in England and Wales, the Uncounted population is, as a proportion of the whole, likely to be larger here than almost anywhere else. National census statistics are equally unreliable, and again exclude the very poorest wherever they are to be found. For instance, it is estimated that between 1.7 per cent and 2.1 per cent of the UK population is excluded from the Family Expenditure Survey (an annual government survey, which, since 1957, has monitored the national rate of family income and expenditure). People living in 'commercial' premises – such as guesthouses, nursing homes for the elderly and disabled, hospitals and prisons – are all excluded from the FES, as are homeless people, those in mobile homes and travelling families who live at 'unrecognised' sites. Almost all are very poor but simply are not counted.

Does it matter? We believe it does. Failure to count those at the bottom means that decisions about the allocation of resources underestimate the scale of the need and particularly disadvantage those areas where there is the highest concentration of Uncounted people – inevitably the poorest communities. The Uncounted therefore either miss out on services altogether or end up competing in the most disadvantaged areas with members of the visible community who are already themselves experiencing multiple deprivation.

So what about solutions? These need to be on a national scale. Were it possible to produce a correct national census, which included *everyone*, the figures would tell a very different story, of a country with a lower national mean income and a higher number of people on low incomes. If we, as a society, are really serious about tackling social exclusion, we need to understand the scale of it. Government initiatives will all be flawed if they are based on an understanding that omits a significant proportion of the most deprived.

We at Community Links think this is important because day after day we see people who are *in* this community but are not a *part* of it. They survive. If we have not hitherto known that they are here, how do they know that we are? If the children begging with cardboard cups outside Stratford tube station have never been to school, their continued absence won't feature in anybody's records and they won't be drawn in to programmes like ours. We can't meet need if we can't measure it or at least appreciate something of its scale.

Our power at Community Links is also, in a sense, our lack of power. We can't deport people or take away their children or their incomes. So we are trusted by those who are most excluded and who lack the skills, knowledge or confidence to access mainstream services. Our outreach work – particularly our Youth programme (the largest in the UK) – is important, but many of our building-based activities are also designed to address the needs of the most marginalised: our Teenage Health project, for example, the Asian women's support group Apna Ghar (see Chapter 8), and various other alternative education programmes.

Of course, we can't do it all. Indeed, often we are not the best people to do it at all. Over the past two decades at Community Links, while becoming aware of the Uncounted residents in East London, we have also become aware of the plethora of informal self-help groups which many of these Uncounted residents have set up to meet their own needs. And, again and again, we have seen how the members of these small, informal groups have transformed their own lives and those of many others, producing extraordinary results that could never have been achieved within the professional bureaucracy. Such groups are not exclusive to East London, of course: as we at Community Links have begun to share our thinking further afield, we have repeatedly encountered other groups, which are doing terrific work on the ground, often among some of our most disadvantaged and marginalised communities, and which are operating entirely below the official waterline. We believe that these groups, which, like the individuals who set them up, are completely Uncounted, are central to any vision of a truly inclusive society. Hence our First Steps training programme, a unique scheme which aims to equip small marginalised groups with the management skills they require to best meet the needs of their own communities. And also our pioneering development of the Social Enterprise Zone (see Chapter 6), which is extending the achievements of government programmes in this area.

Social policy makers now recognise that individual volunteering is a pillar of the welfare state and that in fact almost half of the population is involved in providing essential support (shopping for an elderly housebound neighbour, for example, or helping with childcare) which would otherwise need to be provided by government. When research was undertaken a few years ago, the scale of this 'invisible' contribution was a surprise to almost everybody. We believe that informal community groups are a second pillar of the welfare state – perhaps even more important, but even more invisible.

Does it matter? Again we believe it does. Collectively there is a huge amount of work of this sort going on, and much of it concerns groups and individuals who are excluded from almost every level of organised society – whether it be schools and GPs, or funding opportunities, or dialogue with government, or simply the possibility of gaining wider public awareness.

And yet these groups represent the future. Over the last five to ten years the country's biggest voluntary agencies have been increasingly invited by the Government to deliver a wide range of services and programmes which would formerly have been handled by local and central government agencies. Consequently, the Shaftsbury Society (a children's charity) now derives 90 per cent of its income from government, Mencap 87 per cent, The Leonard Cheshire Foundation 80 per cent (figures taken

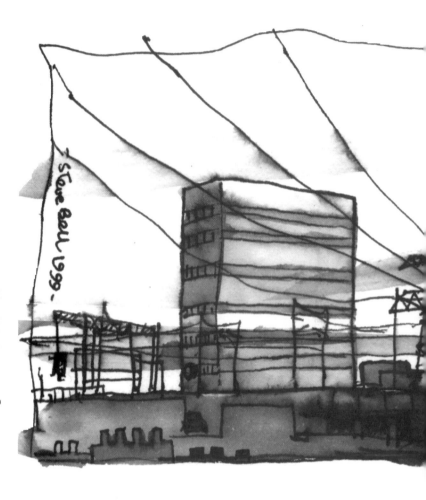

David Robinson Accounting for the Uncounted

Cartoon by Steve Bell

NEW HAM
GATEWAY TO
THE ORIENT

4

from Involuntary Action, published by The Institute of Economic Affairs). And as the professionalised voluntary sector has largely abandoned its founding purpose, so the responsibility for reaching out to the most marginalised in society has shifted from these quasi-statutory, mega charities to the most lively, inspired and well-rooted community groups.

It should be said that, in the last two and a half years, there has been a flurry of new government policies which have sought to tackle the needs of the excluded. We now have a Social Exclusion Unit within the Prime Minister's team at Downing Street and there are new programmes like Sure Start, which are addressing not just the symptoms but also the causes. It is too early, of course, to make judgments about Sure Start at this stage, but the initiative is being closely monitored and the American Head Start programme on which it is based (a scheme set up two decades ago in the United States to provide intensive support for pre-school children and their families) has produced extraordinary results.

Community Links is a committed local partner in all this activity, but still we are troubled by the fear that it is only focusing on the needs of those that we have counted, and that it will be delivered by agencies who lack either the will, the understanding or the capacity to dig deeper. Thus, it may well be possible to achieve all the public sector performance targets and yet still to find, in a decade's time, ten-year-old children begging on Stratford station and mothers buying dog food in the Rathbone market even though they have no dog.

We need to increase our understanding of the Uncounted. In these days of sophisticated data collection and control, are we really unable to count how many people live in our poorest communities? Perhaps if they voted or had a little more spending power we might have found a way of counting them. The fact is, of course, that they could prove to be expensive, and they certainly won't help in the short term with the school and hospital league tables. So we count them out. This means that the performance targets stay manageable and that only the other, less poor people who live here (but who still don't vote or spend as much as the majority of the population) know about the waiting times in casualty – dramatically extended, in this area, by families who don't have and apparently can't get a GP. Most of these Uncounted families would be recognised as homeless if they were recognised at all and many will include children who are receiving no officially supervised education or even basic protection. We need to introduce resource allocation procedures based on methods of data collection that don't exclude the poorest.

At the same time we need to acknowledge that agencies which have failed to connect with the most excluded people in the past aren't the right people to do it now, at least not on their own. And this is where the informal community groups come in. We need first to recognise and then to support these groups. This would bring the highest possible returns. Some of the participants of our First Steps training programme have already achieved extraordinary results. One, the Somali Women's Association, attracted more than 2,000 Somali women to its first meeting. Our priority is to help these groups expand and become more effective – to encourage them to share and inspire good practice, to help them connect the unconnected to mainstream services and to the wider community, but all without diluting the personal experience, the commitment and the dynamism that makes them special.

We also need to help the groups build up links with each other. Our First Steps experience has shown us that connections between groups, often tackling the same issues albeit with completely separate user groups, have a different but equal value to connections from top to bottom. We dream of an informal community 'network' – all sorts of groups linked one to another in small and practical ways, mutually supportive, self-sustaining, practical, visionary, and with deep roots in our most disadvantaged communities, but with branches reaching out to the highest offices in the land. Such a living organism would bear fruit for us all.

Every year the Community Links Ideas Annual features more than 100 schemes and proposals, already working in communities across the UK. Perhaps the Government could help us to build on this scheme by establishing the target of '500 Small Steps' for this Millennium year. One or two of these Steps might be big programmes run from the top down. These would be flagships with the capacity to demonstrate government commitment and affect major change, but which, by definition, because they are controlled from the centre, are likely to be relatively inflexible. Alongside these programmes we might develop a bottom-up approach, encouraging the growth and sharing of small but practical ideas on the ground. We could promote a high-profile national process for drawing in and sharing these ideas. We would have to recognise, of course, that identifying 500 Small Steps is just a beginning. Significant change would take a generation. But even the longest journey begins with individual steps.

And what about the obstacles? Too many new government programmes are driven from the centre. Management by numbers. How do we develop a public service culture which values initiative, encourages flexibility and even, within reasonable bounds, embraces risk? All of this is necessary if we really are to reach the most excluded. Our Social Enterprise Zone (See Chapter 6) is working on some practical ideas, but tackling the culture of public service in the UK is perhaps the biggest challenge. We need secondments, exchanges, the opening up of quangos and a clear message from the Government that doing things differently is not only allowed, it is positively encouraged.

Above all, in the new Millennium we look for a recognition that beyond the excluded there are the Uncounted – ordinary people like you and me, who are working with huge commitment to rebuild lives eroded by ill-health, enforced dislocation or family breakdown and poverty, always poverty. Until we account for the Uncounted, some in our poorest areas will live with a degree of deprivation that most of us would think unthinkable in 21st-century Britain, many will experience community services that are grossly overstretched and thus measurably inferior to comparable services elsewhere and every one of us will live in a society that has turned down, by default or by design, the willing and vibrant contribution of a significant minority.

David Robinson is the director of Community Links

'There is a group of children who sit outside the garages opposite our shop and one night they came over to listen to our music. Otherwise, there's not much for them to do and they just sit there. I want children to grow up with an imagination, I want them to feel included, that they matter'

Eve, 35

Number 5

The British Male at Sixteen

ANDREW O'HAGAN

Darryl Fuller lives in a precarious personal world. He likes Garage music and Kiss FM; he's totally against drugs and plays football and the drums. Since the age of eight, though, he's been excluded from a string of schools. Stuck on the outside of society, he's looking for a way back in

The people on Barking Road are going somewhere. A black woman with a bundle of clothes is padding down to the Laundromat. A guy with drink on his breath is trying to sell a watch. The people in the taxi office are talking into mobile phones. They are making plans for later. The street buses on their way to Stratford and Plaistow come rolling past with people on the top decks deep into novels or the evening paper.

Darryl Fuller is taking up a little corner at Community Links in the old town hall. He sits smiling, at the end of a group of chairs. This is his classroom. He was born on 2 November 1983 in Forest Gate Hospital. When he tries to remember all the houses he has lived in he comes up with a flurry of names: Shaftesbury Road, Upton Park, the Isle of Dogs, Poplar and Beckton, where he lives now with his dad, who is 36, his mother, who is 34, a sister called Sinead, and brothers Daniel and Ricky. They all live in a four-bedroom house with a dog called Chloe. He says when he thinks about it he isn't sure if his mum's 34. 'I don't like to ask.' He doesn't know if the house they live in is rented or bought.

Chloe is an English bull-terrier with a Staffordshire cross. Darryl loves the living daylights out of the dog. We don't know what the dog's first memory is but Darryl's first memory is of being five years old. He was walking down the street and he looked over at some girls and then crashed into a lamp post. The first school he went to was St Stephen's in Green Street. He was excluded after a year. Darryl looks into space when he is trying to remember things. 'Some kid wanted to fight me and I just stuck him,' he says. Then he went to another school in Shaftesbury Road. He was there three weeks, he says, when an Asian kid pulled a knife on him. The kid with the knife was aged ten. Darryl kicked the knife out of his hand and then punched him out. Around then Darryl's mum had another kid and they all moved to a bigger house on the Isle of Dogs. He talks about gangs bullying his sister and he couldn't stand it so he 'flipped'.

'What happens when you flip?'

'One minute I was all calm,' he says, 'and then I turned and I'm out of control. I just don't know what'll happen then. It's always fists – if you can't fight with your fists you can't fight at all. I get mad if someone insults my mum or attacks my sister. I search for people who do that.'

Darryl was 10 when they moved to Beckton. He got expelled from North Beckton School and was later allowed back in. Then he went to Brampton Manor and in the first year he was excluded for fighting. They allowed him back in but he started fighting again and was out by the second year. 'By that time,' he says, 'I was having fights just every other month. At the same time in my life I started bunking. I bunked nearly the whole of my third year and when I was 15 they asked me to leave.'

'Did you have friends?'

'Yeah. Virtually the whole school.'

'Was there anything you liked about school?'

'Yeah. Football. Pottery. Do you want to see my lessons?'

Darryl's doing a thing just now about the different spellings and meanings of words that sound the same. It's all written down in sheets in his folder.

'When you have toothache you have. . . pain.'

'A sheet of glass in a window is a . . . pane.'

'White, or having a colourless face. . . pale.'

'A bucket. . . pail.'

On the arithmetic pages he has shown himself able to add 13 and 34 to make 47. This year he can multiply five by five to make 25. And he can make sense of the proposition that, when seven people eat three bars of chocolate each, then altogether they ate 21 bars.

Darryl likes the idea of everything about him being known and written down. He is the British male at 16. Or is he just one of them? His star sign is Scorpio. He is right-handed. People he tries to avoid are Liz, Bob, Gary and Danny. He likes to watch *Coronation Street*, *EastEnders*, championship wrestling, *South Park*, a music channel called The Box (they have cable in his house) and tons of movies. He is brilliant at Nintendo. There's a PlayStation game he likes called 'Knockabout Kings'. It's a boxing game. 'It's quite hard. I'm the WBA champion un-defeated,' he says. Not only that, but he's brilliant as well at 'Tekun' – a fighting game.

'I expect you are.'

'Yeah. I'm brilliant. I like violent games. I clock it all the way up. I play with my brothers. I've beat everyone there is down my street. One time one of the teachers at one of the schools – 'one time' is a favourite expression of Darryl's – asked him to come in and play drums at assembly. 'It was brilliant,' he says. He would love to own a drum kit of his own and he and some of his friends have been trying to fix up a band. His friend Danny's in the band. He doesn't say anything about Danny being one of his people to avoid.

He likes Garage music. Kiss FM is wicked. He records cool songs off the radio and off the music show on cable. 'Some people say I'm all right on the drums,' he says. West Ham United is his football team. A guy called Denver takes him and some of his mates for football practice down at the ground every Wednesday. Three hours every time. 'It's brilliant,' says Darryl, 'I'm a striker. We've had a good start to the season but now we're playing crap.'

'You mean West Ham?'

'Yeah.'

Darryl says the Prime Minister is called John Blair, or something. When he thinks of what he'd like to do if he was in charge of the country, he says right away that he'd stop racism. ('You could be racist now and down the road end up with a half-caste bird.') He hates drugs as well, he says. 'I have a chance to play for Leyton Orient. I'm trying to calm down and if you do that [drugs], you know what'll happen. It'd be impossible to get rid of drugs but I'd like to. I've got a mate who takes drugs and he just looks so ill.'

'Are you really not interested in drugs?'

'No way,' he says, 'they're for mugs.' He smiles.

'Really? None at all?'

He smiles again. 'You're probably just saying that 'cos you take them,' he says. He paused for ages before saying the third thing he'd do if he ruled the country. 'I know,' he says, 'I would sort charity out. If people need help they should get it – you know – support and that.'

Listening to Darryl, you find yourself able both to admire him and to worry. He lives in a precarious personal world. He is only beginning to know what he can trust; he is only beginning to want to be trustworthy himself. No one would find Darryl an impossible proposition now: he is growing up likeable, with more personality than charm, and more charm than free-floating anger.

But he needs protection in his youth. He needs only to be talked away from his difficult traits: given lessons, a football coach, a number of small tasks, a weekend job at Booker's cash-and-carry. Darryl Fuller wants nothing more than the smart benefits of an able community. He needs to be part of something that is slightly bigger than he is himself. At Community Links, on Barking

Road, something of the sort has gripped him. The only worry is, can he stick it? Can he give himself up to the better thing?

On a typical day Darryl is woken up by his mum at nine a.m.

'Yeah, I'm brilliant. I love violer

He gets washed and might eat something and if his mum's busy he'll iron his own shirt. Then he gets on a bike and cycles to Community Links, where he learns the difference between 'pain' and 'pane', and where there's an environment that allows him to feel he's going somewhere. As well as learning things he also does odd jobs around the building – 'helping old people down-stairs with their tea and that' – and he sees the time just rolling away with all he's got to do now. 'People up here got respect for me,' he says. 'They know who I am. They leave me to get on with my work. I get on with everybody now.'

Darryl says he can't think of anyone to blame about his school-days. He says if he's honest it was him. 'I'm young,' he says, 'I don't know how my life will go. I just want nothing bad to happen. I just want to be myself.' He sometimes gets frustrated because he wants things to go faster. He wants to be better quicker. He has learned a lot more than he ever did at school, though. There are only six or seven people in his class at Community Links.

ames. I clock it all the way up.'

He's been on planes. He went skiing in the Alps. He went to Lourdes with some folk who couldn't walk. Darryl doesn't go to church but his mum goes and she's a Catholic. 'I don't believe in God,' he says. 'They say he made us and I say, who made Him? They say, Adam and Eve, and they say, the apes made them, and I say, who made the apes?' But if he had to die for anything, then he thinks it should be his family. If he had to name two things he hates, he'd say it was school and muggers. His heroes are his mum and his dad and his nan. He'd like to have a silver Porsche Boxer Turbo. He has no fear of cars, even though he was in a crash once, with his dad. Fifteen stitches in his head. It was somebody else's fault: they jumped the lights. But, anyway, he wants to forget all that and wouldn't mind it if one day he lived in a mansion. He's not going steady with a girl but he has a few girlfriends he sees all the time. He says that girls admire him for the muscles on his

5

stomach although he doesn't even work out.

Outside the strip-lighted classroom other people are coming into the building for classes and meetings and coffee and tea. You can hear music starting up for a dance class downstairs. All over the place the sense rises up of an effort being made; a sense of things being overcome and time being invested. As well as all that there's the sound of people having a laugh. The sound of laughter travelling over troubles and up the stairs and along the corridor to where I'm sitting with Darryl Fuller.

For money Darryl relies on his mum. She gives him a few quid here and there. So does his dad. But one of these days he's going to get a part-time job at Booker's in Beckton; he would like it if he could have more money for drums or clothes or that Porsche Boxer Turbo. He is wearing a light green Ben Sherman shirt. He is very pleased with his hooded top from Paul Smith. His trousers cost 60 quid. His favourite shoes are Kickers and the ones he is wearing are brown and comfy. He wears white socks and he thinks that socks are important. There's a barber's called Geezers where he gets his hair cut; his brown hair is cut into a kind of wedge but he says it's not a wedge, it's called curtains. He says he's been shaving since he was 14 but his skin looks brand new.

Darryl sticks his tongue out when he makes a joke. When you ask him what he thinks of the police he begins to look a bit shifty. 'They do their job don't they? But I hate the way they pull up my mates just 'cause they've got bald heads.' He used to have a bald head himself but then he got into the pop singer Peter Andre who has hair hanging over his face: curtains. He likes the way there are all different kinds of people at Community Links. They're not all the same: they have their own traits and looks and things going on, just like he has. Darryl says that some of the people who come to Barking Road have worse problems than him, but he wants to respect them. He's learned to get on.

'I feel quite sorted out in my head,' he says. 'If I wanted to be a gangster I'd know what to do. But I don't want that. Not now. I don't get off on knowing villains or anything.' He slumps in the chair, smiles in a lop-sided way, and looks around the room where he says good things have happened for him. 'I'd like to have a family some day,' he says.

Darryl's eyes are hazel. He is five foot five. He is 16 years old and proud of it, thank you. His favourite colour is claret. He walks down the stairs of Community Links smiling at everyone and making jokes. The people he meets seem glad he's on his way. The last I see of him he picks up his bike and wheels it towards the doors. It is dark outside. He smiles a big smile as he hops on his bike and heads into Barking Road. Like the rest of the world out there, he is at his best with somewhere to go.

On the way out I look at a piece of paper. It carries the words of Betty Young, an 86-year-old woman who helped set up Community Links at an East Ham shop in 1978. 'The shop was damp and it smelt of coal tar from when the chemist used to be there,' she said. 'There was always boys there, at first three and then more, boys who should have been at school. I know some of them were in trouble but they were always good to me. Gradually we got things going. I remember thinking, I've seen a lot of bad things but this is a good.'

The 86-year-old's words – on a cold night last October – seemed almost to propel the British Male at 16 on his way up Barking Road.

Andrew O'Hagan is the film critic of the *Daily Telegraph*. His first novel, *Our Fathers* (Faber & Faber, £16.99), was shortlisted for the 1999 Booker Prize

5

'New projects like the Excel Centre, the Channel Tunnel Rail Link and the City Airport are all useful, but they ought to be giving something back to local people. A tax could be paid by those businesses that directly benefit from these developments (hotels, cab firms, shops), say 1-2 per cent of their increased profits. This could be used to create a permanent flow of funding for community projects'

Greg, 41

Number 6

As Easy as 1⇧2⇧3

MATTHEW SMERDON

Britain's first Social Enterprise Zone provides an exciting model for the regeneration of our inner cities

In a book of visions, we begin with a view. From the roof of the Community Links building in Canning Town, you can see all sorts of impressive new developments going on in East London. You may see a gleaming new Jubilee Line train on its way to the Dome, via the recently completed, futuristic station at Canning Town. You may also see a passenger jet coming in to land at City Airport, which is itself just the other side of the docks from the construction site of London's largest new conference venue. Standing over all this is 1 Canada Square, the 50-storey show-piece tower at the heart of Canary Wharf, the Business Enter-prise Zone which is one of the largest commercial property developments in Europe.

But look a bit closer, and you will realise that you are also look-ing out over part of one of the most extensive areas of urban deprivation in Europe. This area has experienced every state-sponsored regeneration initiative since the 1960s, from Urban Aid to City Challenge to Single Regeneration Budget. Yet, for all this, and for all the bright new stations and buildings, people still live here with the day-to-day implications of long-term and multiple forms of poverty, which touch every area of life: health, education, work, travel, leisure, communications, insurance and safety.

The statistics are revealing. In Newham, total spending by the public sector accounts for 65-75 per cent of the local economy (in more wealthy areas of the country the percentage would be nearer 40 per cent). Of this public sector money in Newham, 98 per cent is spent on mainstream maintenance programmes, such as the welfare and housing budgets, while only two per cent is dedicated to regeneration. One example of this glaring disparity between mainstream and regeneration expenditure is a new regeneration project based in a group of neighbourhoods, to the north of the Community Links building, in Plaistow and West Ham. This group of neighbourhoods has recently been selected as a Pathfinder area for the New Deal for Communities initiative, which will bring in some £50 million over the next ten years. It sounds like a large amount of money. However, if benefit payments remain at their current level, 24 times that amount will be spent over the same period of time in this area on benefit payments alone.

The problem is that the public sector money which is flowing into Newham is being used to tackle the *symptoms* of deprivation rather than its *causes*. Clearly, the two per cent of the budget currently spent on regeneration is not enough. But what if we could harness the potential of the other 98 per cent more effectively? This is precisely what Community Links has been trying to do, with its pioneering work on the development of Social Enterprise Zones (SEZ). A pilot project is already underway in Newham, and funding has been secured to put this first national Zone in place.

The SEZ concept builds on the experience of the Business Enterprise Zones, introduced in the early 1980s, which tested how far industrial and commercial activity could be encouraged by removing certain fiscal burdens and removing, or streamlining, certain statutory or administrative controls. This flexible approach was successful in the business arena, so why not try it in the social one? Currently, statutory rules and procedures governing public sector spending can prevent existing mainstream resources from being used effectively. In a SEZ, a consortium of agencies and local people can seek licence to flex these rules wherever this will make a difference. The ultimate idea is that the partners in the consortium will sign a ten-year commitment to work together, not just in the management of fringe activities, but in radically reviewing and subsequently delivering mainstream programmes.

The SEZ process is composed of three stages, collected

together under a simple, catch-all term, **1**⇨**2**⇨**3**:

1 Mobilising local people, the public sector and private sector organisations

A SEZ is driven by a distinctive way of working, designed to be lean and catalytic, which is totally dependent on active community involvement. In these early stages of putting the SEZ into practice in our area, a multi-disciplinary team has already been brought together as the SEZ Development Group. This team is offering the SEZ strategic direction and advice, and forming the beginnings of a network that will take us to the heart of the community and the state. Being effective is not rocket science, but it does necessitate taking a new approach, which recognises that deprivation operates on many levels and cannot be effectively tackled by focusing exclusively on any single one of them. We need to work away from excuses for why things cannot be done, towards ideas of how they can.

2 Generating and gathering innovative ideas for changing rules and procedures to create flexibility in the way public sector resources are used

The SEZ is based on the fundamental premise that both the local community and the agencies delivering welfare services in the area have good ideas. As experience shows, but social policy rarely reflects, those people living and working with particular problems are the ones who know best how to solve them. It is important here to realise that the best ideas need not be complicated. In Newham a process called 'What if...?' is now underway, designed to gather ideas for change. Like the visions in this book, these ideas are intended to be positive statements of how things could be different rather than comments focusing on what is wrong.

Of course, there are many good ideas already up and running all over the country and beyond. People from Liverpool, South Wales,

Glasgow, Brighton, Newcastle and other London boroughs, as well as the USA, have been in touch with us to offer examples of initiatives which are working in their areas and could work even better given the **1⇨2⇨3** opportunity.

3 Ensuring effective mechanisms are in place to develop, test and share these ideas

Some progress can be made at the local level, on a voluntary basis, by public agencies simply deciding to work together. However, freedom to think and act strategically and creatively requires the active encouragement and support of individuals throughout government, the civil service and public sector agencies. In so doing, the principle that the state and its machinery are forces for progress is reaffirmed, for if state machinery has put rules and procedures in place, it can also be the vehicle to remove them.

The public sector needs to feel safe with SEZ initiatives, and some careful work will have to be done to develop appropriate frameworks of accountability. That said, if rules and procedures are not changed, it is legitimate to ask why not, who is in control and for whose benefit? Partner organisations can expect to achieve savings if they work together to meet the aims of the SEZ, even though they will be providing a service as good as, or better than, the current one. Savings of public expenditure arising from the SEZ process should be made available for reinvestment within the SEZ during its lifetime.

At the heart of **1⇨2⇨3** is an effort to redefine how the state manages its resources in response to local communities, calling for changes in rules and procedures which do not work. In so doing, **1⇨2⇨3** seeks to bring regeneration on to the mainstream agenda of public sector services. Employment/Health/Education Action Zones, Single Regeneration Budget, New Deal for Communities, etc, can stack up on one another and risk perpetuating a regeneration strategy that just tinkers at the margins. Through its detailed and sustained questioning of the rules and procedures which govern the way state policy on social and economic progress is applied, a SEZ seeks to reassert the principle that the state should be judged by the extent to which it serves the needs of *all* its people.

People increasingly talk of the need to be risk-taking. Yet it need not always be as dramatic as this. A SEZ will use existing resources, it will just use them better. The SEZ vision calls for a welfare state which is a genuine ladder out of poverty, where welfare payments do not just keep people on lower rungs, but instead act as a vehicle for them to climb up and out of poverty for good. No one is suggesting that any public, private or voluntary sector body has ever set out to *create* poverty; the idea behind the SEZ is simply to change the rules and procedures which sometimes have that effect.

We are very excited about the prospects for the SEZ pilot in Newham, and would welcome your input, ideas and support. We picture a society that enables every individual to fulfil their potential. Achieving this? It's as easy as **1**⇨**2**⇨**3**.

Matthew Smerdon is a research and development worker at Community Links. The other members of the SEZ Development Group are **Frances Clarke** (Community Links), **Greg Clarke** (Greater London Enterprise Ltd), **Mavis Fernandes** (Community Links), **Donald Hirsch** (Joseph Rowntree Foundation), **Stephen Jacobs** (Stratford Development Partnership), **George Leahy** (East London and City Health Authority), **John Low**, (Joseph Rowntree Foundation), **Richard Reeves** (*The Observer*), **Charles Richardson** (3 i), **David Robinson** (Community Links), **Matthew Taylor** (Institute for Public Policy Research), **Katharine Woods** (London Borough of Newham), **Ian Woolford** (New Deal for Communities)

Cartoon by Steve Bell

'I know someone who is trying to start her own business but she can't save enough from her benefits to build up the capital to give the business a chance of working. As soon as she makes any money to invest in the business, they cut her benefits so she has to spend her savings to get by and then go back on benefits. Why not let her claim benefits at the same time as working so that she could invest some money in her business?'

Nicky, 27

Number 7
In Conversation with Alya Din

GORDON BROWN

We always complain that politicians don't ever really talk to the people they are supposed to be helping. Here, the Chancellor of the Exchequer talks to Alya Din, a New Deal trainee, about her experience of the youth employment scheme the Government set up in 1997

GB: You've got a wonderful name, Alya, A.L.Y.A.

AD: Thank you.

GB: It's a very nice name.

AD: It's the name of an Arabian Princess.

GB: Is it? We must call you Princess Alya.

AD: That's what I do prefer. (Laughter).

GB: You're going to write an article are you? Based on what I say?

AD: Yes, so here are the questions. When you were setting up the New Deal Training Scheme, what problems were you trying to solve?

GB: I came from Fife in Scotland and we had, at one stage, 30,000 miners and we've now got less than a thousand, and you could see how for the young people the obvious thing to do, 20 years ago and 10 years ago, was to find a job in mining. But there are no jobs left in that, so people now realise that they have got to get skills and qualifications, and if they don't have skills or get training then they're not going to get jobs that pay well. So what we are trying to do is help the sort of young people that I meet in my constituency who maybe, 20 years ago, would have gone into mining, or maybe in your area would have gone on to work in engineering or something. That's what the New Deal is about. If people are unemployed when they are young, they will tend to be unemployed when they are older and if they are long-term unemployed, unemployed for lots of months and lots of years, they will tend to be unemployed for even longer periods of time when they get older. So we thought we would help the thousands of young people who are unemployed into working. We taxed the utility companies, gas and electricity, we took five billion pounds – five thousand million pounds – in tax, so that we could provide a service for young people to get jobs. That's the inspiration behind the New Deal. It's *wrong* for any young person not to have anything to do. I think it's *wrong* if we provide the opportunity for people to stay at home and do nothing as well.

AD: I'm a 22-year-old university graduate, brought up in north-east London. Would you say that I'm a typical New Deal trainee?

GB: I think you're very well qualified and we've got to help you get a job. We are now in a situation where there are probably a million vacancies in the British economy – there are about 200,000 in London and the South East – so what we've got to do is to help the people without jobs to find the jobs that need to be filled. We're doing a number of things that I hope will help, not only helping people get more skills but getting people more inform-ation about the jobs that are available.

AD: In the end, though, someone has got to do the dead-end jobs, like stacking shelves in Sainsbury's. What do you do if no one wants to stack shelves in Sainsbury's?

GB: When I was a student, like you've been a student, I took any job that was available so that I could get work and have some income. If you start in what some people call a starter job, it doesn't mean that it's a dead-end. It means it's a start for you to do the next job, and then the next job, and then the next job. We want people to see jobs as a ladder of opportunities. And that's why we have implemented a policy where there's a min-imum wage.

AD: I get £56 a week on the New Deal: how do you expect me to spend this?

GB: Well that's up to you. (Laughter). How *do* you spend it?

AD: Well, what I mean is, when you set out the amount, how did you decide that £56 was enough?

GB: Everybody starts somewhere and that was what we could afford, having taxed the utilities to get money to pay for employment programmes for a whole parliament.

AD: Do you think it's enough to live on?

GB: Well, I think that it's what we could afford as a government, but obviously you will want to move on and get a job and then get a better income and perhaps get an even better job with an even better income… so you've got to see it as a start.

AD: How would *you* spend £56?

GB: Well, I would… well, the obvious starting point is food, isn't it? And then you've got to work out from there. Do you stay with relatives or at home?

AD: Yes I live at home with my mum.

GB: And she's helpful, is she?

AD: Yes, very.

GB: We've got to see everything as a start to the next thing, which will lead to the next thing. I don't want anybody to feel they're in dead-end jobs. Remember, ten years ago, there were almost three million people unemployed in Britain, now there are far less. There's lower unemployment in Britain than there has been for 20 years. It's not true now to say there are no opportunities – though obviously we want to get the opportunities in the right place at the right time for the people who need them.

AD: How do you budget your own personal life?

GB: I don't budget it. (Laughter). Well, I try not to spend more than I have.

AD: As a member of the Cabinet, you must have most things paid for you. Do you ever have to spend any of your own money?

GB: Oh yes, all the time. I don't have most things paid for me; I buy most things. (Laughter). And, as you must know, when Labour came into government we froze the pay of Cabinet ministers for the first year – first *two* years.

AD: Going back to the New Deal, one of the things my friends and I have found is that it is very inflexible. As part of our six-month training, we are obliged to do an NVQ Level 2 in information and technology, a basic computer skills course. I feel that in my case it's a waste of time – I'm actually also attending an evening class in website design on the Internet, so I have quite an advanced knowledge of computers, but I am not allowed to do any other course. Why is this not permitted?

GB: You must write and protest and we'll see what we can do. If you've already got the qualification and you say you want to do something else and get another qualification, then you should.

AD: But a lot of us have asked for this and we were told there is no way that we can do anything else.

GB: Well then I shall take that up, and I'll ask questions about that, and I'll get Stephen Timms, your local MP, to write to you. Obviously, it's far better if people can get the benefit they need.

AD: It also seems to me that the New Deal is very much geared towards administration work. Is this the case?

GB: No, because there are a number of different parts of the New Deal. There's a New Deal option where you work with voluntary organisations, a New Deal where you can be taken on by private organisations, and that can be anything. There's a New Deal that's an environmental task force and a New Deal that's a training course, providing places at college – so it's not necessarily the case that it's administrative work at all… although there are a lot of jobs in administration at the moment.

AD: And what if someone wants to be a stuntman?

GB: Well, they should be able to qualify. We had a debate about this, about whether musicians and people training to be singers could qualify for the New Deal – and eventually we decided that we could help. But I don't know about stuntmen.

AD: Do you think there are other ways in which the New Deal could be improved?

GB: We are trying to extend it to the long-term unemployed – that's adults. We're then extending it to lone parents. And we're about to introduce new measures to help disabled people. We're also about to introduce a new measure for the over 50s, people who lost a job and need to get another job but want to have particular help to get back into work.

AD: Have you ever been unemployed?

GB: I *was* unemployed after I left university, but not for long – a few weeks. But remember, unemployment has gone down. There are 600,000 new jobs since we came into government... What I'm trying to persuade people is that we can get a situation where, instead of assuming that three million or two million or even one million people are unemployed, we actually give most people who want to work a chance to work.

AD: If, after six months on the New Deal, I don't find a job, what do you suggest I do?

GB: We want to give you all the help that we can to find a job. Are you applying for lots of jobs at the moment?

AD: Yes, all the time.

GB: Where do you find them advertised – in the 'job centres'? Or do you find them advertised in newspapers?

AD: Yes, newspapers.

GB: And have you had some interviews recently?

AD: Yes.

GB: And you're still waiting to hear?

AD: Yes.

GB: Well, you've got lots of applications in so I hope something turns up. There are opportunities and I hope you can benefit from them.

AD: It seems that in some ways, as far as the Government is concerned, offering training schemes to young unemployed people who *want* a job is easy. What do you do about people who *don't* want to do anything?

GB: If you're a young person who is unemployed and you're claiming benefit and we're providing lots of opportunities to get either work or training or work experience or education then I don't think you should get benefit unconditionally... if you just stay at home and do nothing.

AD: But there are people who just don't want to work.

GB: Then we've got to help them get back into work and coach them if necessary.

AD: But how do you motivate them?

GB: We've been looking at different programmes around the country, and actually Community Links does a lot of work, and we obviously want to find people who will help people who are either demotivated or disillusioned or who found their experience of college, or not college, unhelpful to them. Or people who have perhaps had a problem with crime or drugs or something. We want to provide a helper, a coach or a mentor, or whatever you call it, who will help... So gradually we'll get through to people. I don't want any young person to sit at home and say there's no opportunity because there *is* opportunity. And I don't want us just to pay out benefit and say, 'We'll forget about you but we'll give you a few pounds a week.' I want to say, 'Look, we'll help you, we'll give you some more financial help, we'll give you a coach or someone to train you, we'll give you help to get a qualification – but you've got to take up the opportunity, you can't just stay at home doing absolutely nothing.

AD: One of the things me and my friends have found is that the benefits system can be quite bureaucratic and rigid. For example, when I was temping, sometimes I'd work on an assignment which lasted five or six weeks, then have three weeks without work, and it didn't seem worth my while signing on because you have to fill in a 36-page form every time, wait for hours, then wait another few weeks before a cheque comes through. After doing that two or three times, it put me off and I didn't bother going to sign on. Why don't you reform that system so that it is a little more helpful?

GB: Well maybe we should get you to redesign that – on the Internet! (Laughter).

AD: You fill in the form and sign on; then, after doing a job for a while, when you go back to sign on you have to fill in another whole form again.

GB: Do you not have a copy of the form you filled in in the first place?

AD: They don't keep them – why don't they?

GB: Maybe because there are lots of forms around. I don't know. Obviously you don't want to spend lots of time filling in forms – you want a *job*.

AD: Why can't they be more helpful?

GB: Can you not keep a copy yourself?

AD: They don't allow that.

GB: Well, we'll have to have a look at this. Of course, the important thing for you is that you don't want to have to fill in the form at all, you just want to keep working.

AD: Do you like *your* job?

GB: Some of it.

AD: But, do you really enjoy it or do you do it just for the money?

GB: I would do it if there was no money, but obviously I've got to survive.

AD: Have you ever wanted to be prime minister?

GB: I'm quite happy doing the job that I do.

AD: So you've never wanted to be prime minister?

GB: Don't know. We'll see.

AD: What's the most extravagant thing you have ever bought?

GB: Bought? I don't know. My house, I suppose. (Laughter)

AD: Moving on to a more serious issue, how realistic are the current moves, Net Aid, for example, to try and cancel all world debt?

GB: This is very important. If we can reduce a country's debt and at the same time make sure money goes not into military expenditure or corrupt expenditure, but into health and education and eliminating poverty, that is something that is very worth doing. And to do it in the Millennium is very important as well – we are going to wipe off a hundred billion dollars, *a hundred thousand million dollars*.

AD: What are your visions for the Millennium?

GB: (Roars of laughter, then pause). One of Britain where there's opportunity for all and where everybody makes a contribution. A world where people feel they are free from fear: fear of poverty, fear of violence, as well as fear of ignorance and fear of unemployment. I think if the Millennium teaches us anything it's that, if people come together and pursue high ideals, then they can achieve a great deal. And that's not politicians, it's the people.

AD: Do you think, in my lifetime, I, or someone like me, could become chancellor of the exchequer?

GB: Yes. Yes, I hope so – there's never been a woman chancellor...

Alya Din, 22, is a university graduate. Last year she did a six-month work placement at Community Links on the New Deal

'I got involved in a small local community group. It boosted my morale and sense of belonging. Through making contact with people in the same situation, I was learning about needs and rights and I found a positive out of what could have been a negative'

Jamila, 17

LOUISE FRANCE

Number 8

Breaking the Silence

In the 16 years since it was set up, Apna Ghar has provided a lifeline for Asian women in East London suffering from domestic violence

There is a popular saying in Asian culture. It goes: 'A woman leaves her father's house in a wedding carriage; she leaves her husband's house in a coffin.' It is repeated so often that people barely register what they are saying any more. Yet when Sudarshan Bhuhi hears the phrase, she feels sick to her stomach. She would be happy if she never heard it again.

A gentle, chic woman in her early forties, Sudarshan runs Apna Ghar (which translates as Our Home), one of the few support groups in Britain for Asian women who have suffered domestic violence. She knows that the 'wedding carriage' proverb is more than a harmless ditty: it signifies just how little power Asian women have within their marriages. And it is a chilling indication of what can happen to a woman if she does show any independence.

Four new cases arrive on Apna Ghar's books every day. There are the wives whose husbands keep them under lock and key, 24 hours a day; the women who are hit by their husbands (and often their mothers-in-law and sisters-in-law too); and the young women who call from Heathrow airport just minutes before they are due to be forced on to a flight to Pakistan for an arranged marriage. Unofficial figures indicate that as many as 60 per cent of women in Asian households experience abuse, be it physical, sexual or emotional.

Domestic violence is a complex issue in any culture. In Asian culture it is especially so. Violence is often exacted for reasons of 'honour'. For instance, if a woman is seen to rebel against a forced marriage, her family may use verbal or physical abuse to keep her in line for fear that the rest of the community will find out. 'Many, many Asian women don't realise they're being abused because they think it's "normal",' says Sudarshan, a mother of four who is now in a happy second marriage. 'Or they'll blame the violence on their karma. "It's a Karmic thing," they'll say. "I must have done something in my previous lives and now I'm paying for it. If I don't pay for it now I will have to go through it again, so I might as well pay for it now to have a better life in my next reincarnation." '

The problem is that the abuse tends to come from several quarters, not just from a woman's husband. As Sudarshan explains: 'The wife is traditionally caught between the demands of her husband's family, her own family and her children. Everyone, including her mother-in-law, has power over her. In fact, the mother-in-law may have been abused herself, but it makes no difference. In Asian families prestige comes with age, the older you are the more respect you command. For the first time in her life, a mother-in-law will feel powerful, in control. She thinks, "I was abused and now it's someone else's turn. All my life I have done what other people have told me. Finally other people are doing what I say." '

Women from all parts of society are affected. 'It's just as bad for the middle classes,' explains Sudarshan. 'Often women who have good careers – solicitors, teachers – don't dare tell anyone that they are abused. It's as if, because they come from a well-known family, they are even more ashamed of what is going on behind closed doors.'

Apna Ghar was set up in 1984, and has provided a lifeline for thousands of women since. All the more remarkable, then, that it started almost by accident. Sixteen years ago Sudarshan was a 27-year-old secretary working on the reception desk at Community Links. At 10 o'clock in the morning a Pakistani woman with two children, aged around eight and nine, came running through the door and started beating her hands on the desk.

Quickly, the woman's story came tumbling out. She'd been in a violent relationship for a long time – punching, hitting, abusive language. Because she was so scared that she'd say the wrong thing, she barely spoke to her husband. But the day before, she said, he had started to attack her while she cooked samosas. He had picked up the frying-pan, full of boiling oil, and had been on the brink of throwing it at her. 'And then I knew that one day he would kill me,' she told Sudarshan. 'I knew we had to get out.'

She had fled with her children to her sister's house but it had not been difficult for her husband to track her down. Now he was threatening to take the children. 'To tell you the truth,' says Sudarshan, looking back, 'I didn't know what to do. All I knew was that this woman had seen my face – the face of an Asian woman – and thought I'd be able to help. I got on to the phone to the local solicitors and demanded that we get help. By two in the afternoon we had travelled across London by bus and tube and reached the High Court. By 2.30 p.m, her children were made wards of court. The *difference* those hours made to her life after all those years of marriage. She suddenly felt that she could do anything. Finally she realised that her husband couldn't hurt her.'

Sudarshan never heard from the woman again. But word went round the local Asian community. The next week another woman came up to reception and whispered that she had problems in her marriage. As more and more women began to turn up, it became obvious that there was a need for a more formal support network. So Sudarshan set up a Tuesday morning drop-in group.

To begin with, the true role of Apna Ghar (the name was chosen by the women who attended those original Tuesday morning sessions) was kept secret. The sessions were billed as sewing classes and English lessons so that wives and daughters had a safe alibi for turning up. 'Back then I didn't have a clue what I was doing,' remembers Sudarshan. 'All I knew was that these women needed each other and this was providing a way for them to meet. In two months there were 40 women attending regularly.'

Today Apna Ghar is no longer in hiding. Most people in the Asian community know what its role is – even if they disapprove. Besides Sudarshan, there are two full-time members of staff, two part-time ones and three group workers, as well as various volunteers. They run a help line, a drop-in service and a home-visiting scheme (for which they have no funding). They also liaise with courts and solicitors when women need help with legal proceedings. And there is an after-school group for young girls, a single mothers' group and a special help group for Asian women over 55.

Research shows that many women, regardless of their cultural background, stay in violent relationships because, after years and years of abuse, they lose the ability to make decisions for themselves. For Asian women the situation is even more difficult. Raised in a culture where family and home mean everything, they simply do not have the experience to cope with life outside. For many of them, just paying the gas bill or the television licence on their own is an achievement after years of subservience. Living independently takes a huge amount of courage.

Education is the key to progress, says Sudarshan. Teaching the perpetrators that violence is not the long-term solution to problems. Teaching women that being hit or punched or ignored is not acceptable. 'Often I will ask women if they have been abused and they will reply "no". Then, when I go through the list, it's a different story. "Did he threaten you?" "Yes." "Did he kick you?" "Yes." "Did he push you around?" "Yes." "Did he have sex with you against your will?" "Yes." '

Sometimes a woman will realise that violence is wrong but she won't understand that mental abuse is just as debilitating. Sudarshan tells the story of one woman who rang early one morning, just as she had entered the office. '"The police have given me your telephone number," said the voice at the end of the line. "I have to get to you. I can't talk." When the woman arrived, she had two little children with her. You could feel the distress she was suffering and tell, from the way the children were crying and the clothes they wore, that perhaps they hadn't been at home the night before.'

Later, seated in the quiet room that Apna Ghar keeps for one-to-one consultations, Sudarshan carefully persuaded the woman that she could now talk without fear of recrimination. The woman told her of how she'd been married in Pakistan and was now living in Newham. And how, ever since her arrival in Britain, her husband had kept her under lock and key. She lived with her husband, mother-in-law, sister-in-law and brother-in-law. There was a lock on both sides of the front door. If the family left her, they would lock the door on the outside. She was effectively imprisoned. But for a long time, because she was not allowed to speak to anyone outside the family, she had thought her life was normal. That this was how women lived in Britain.

For three years she had simply moved from room to room, cooking and cleaning. Any letters to her parents were checked; any letters she received were kept. Her parents never knew what she was suffering. Nor did she want to tell them what was going on because she had younger sisters who were themselves approaching the marrying age. If she had had to leave to go back to Pakistan, she would have let her own family down.

'Then, a breakthrough,' says Sudarshan, 'the day before she called me at Community Links, she had come downstairs and realised that her mother-in-law had forgotten to take the key out of the lock on the inside. In a split second, she grabbed the children, opened the door and ran. She made her way to the local police station and the authorities did what they often do now: they called Apna Ghar.'

Not surprisingly, many of the more traditional members of the Asian community feel threatened by the work that Apna Ghar does. Fund-raising is not easy. When Sudarshan stands with her collection box in East Ham High Street, people often come up to harangue her. 'We'd help you if it was the local hospital,' they say. 'But not this. Why are you washing our dirty clothes in public? This has been going on for centuries. Why do something now?'

Sudarshan, however, is an optimist. She believes that the cycle of abuse in Asian culture can be broken by persuasion and negotiation. Apna Ghar does not have the resources to house everyone that it would like to. But at least now Asian women in East London know that there is a place where they can go to get help if they need it. Sudarshan sees the future of Apna Ghar as empowering Asian women in general. 'If we can help women feel powerful, their children will feel powerful too. Boys will grow up respecting women and knowing that violence is wrong. Girls will grow up understanding their rights.'

Louise France is editor of the Real Life section of the *Independent on Sunday*

'I can talk to people in Brazil on the Internet but I want to know my own neighbours and feel safe enough to be able to go out and leave my keys in the door'

Paula, 21

Number 9

In Celebration of Ordinariness

STEPHEN JACOBS

Let the future Canning Town be a place its inhabitants can be proud of – an ordinary place, with ordinary fortunes and misfortunes

Accustomed, average, conventional, established, everyday, familiar, modest, popular, common, traditional, usual, not exceptional – *ordinary*.

Most people's aspirations for the Millennium are about having the biggest, the best and the most expensive of everything. For us in Canning Town that is not good enough – we want all that is ordinary, all year round. We are fed up with having extraordinary levels of crime, extraordinary problems with housing, extraordinary health and life chances for children and extraordinary results at school.

We want ordinary jobs, to which ordinary people can aspire – jobs of real worth, with adequate pay, and a chance of progression – not the low-paid, part-time jobs that we have become used to. We want ordinary housing in Canning Town, houses with gardens front and back, and pitched roofs – not the sort of problem-ridden, systems-built housing that was erected in times when architects and planners had their way. We want ordinary health facilities, the kind they have in ordinary areas, with well-maintained, up-to-date GP surgeries and hospitals. We want ordinary schools which reflect the ordinary results achieved elsewhere. And, most importantly, we want ordinary teachers who will stay in the area for more than a few months, and teach our children to want and expect better for themselves and their families. In short, we want an ordinary area much like many others.

We want other people to see us as ordinary; we want civil servants and local bureaucrats to see us as ordinary. We don't want to be stuck with labels such as 'socially excluded', 'inner city', 'sink estates', with all the stigmas that come with them.

We want other people to talk to us like ordinary people and not to treat us as some kind of social experiment. We want to be able to exercise our own ordinary rights to decide what is best for us. Please stop coming back, time and time again, with more 'initiatives'. We would have a lot of initiative ourselves if only we were allowed to use it.

Achieving this ordinariness will not be easy. It will take time. It also means that we will have to take on ordinary responsibilities for looking after ourselves and our community. For ordinariness is not something which can be imposed from above – it has to be arrived at organically, to be generated from within. Here, then, is my vision for the Millennium.

In the years to come:

■ The queues at Canning Town Post Office will be made up of people queuing to buy stamps and to deposit savings, rather than people collecting benefits.

■ Our schools will be overflowing, not because of a shortage of school places, but because out-of-borough children will want to attend them.

■ Our residents will no longer be boycotted by hire-purchase firms, and, as far as insurance companies are concerned, a Canning Town address will carry no more stigma than any other ordinary area.

■ Marks & Spencer will have opened several new Metro stores to cash in on the increased amount of disposable income among Canning Town residents.

■ The council will have rejected a planning application for a new indoor Sports & Leisure facility on the grounds that Canning Town is already well provided for with two or three centres.

■ Health statistics will show that living in Canning Town is no more 'unhealthy' than any other ordinary area, and that there has been a marked decline in the traditional killers of East Londoners, namely heart disease, cancer and TB.

- Canning Town's Thames-side location, and its excellent tube, rail and river transport systems, will have been exploited by a huge number of riverside residential and commercial developments, providing yet more jobs for the highly skilled local workforce.

- London City Airport will have become 'Canning Town Airport', a name considered by its new owners to have more cachet than the 'London City' tag.

- The Government will be concerned about the alarming population drift from West to East London.

- Canning Town and its surrounding neighbourhoods will be suffering from over-employment, with local wages at 150% of the national average.

- A survey of local children will indicate a majority wishing to gain high-status and high-wage jobs.

- Canning Town will be voted Best Environmental Area in England (the A13 having recently been buried).

- By 2010 at the latest, Canning Town will have expunged both absolute poverty and, more importantly, the poverty of expectations which has held back its residents for so long.

Above all, it will be a place which will look ordinary to you, but not to us. It will be a place where we are proud to live and work and, yes, even play. It will be a stop on the Jubilee Line, where people passing by may look at each other and say, 'Umm…Canning Town, pretty ordinary isn't it?'

I can't wait.

Stephen Jacobs is chief executive of the Stratford Development Partnership

Cartoon by Steve Bell

9

'It only takes a few people to stop dropping litter for other people to stop too. It could start with people agreeing to clean outside their home. It doesn't take much time. We could have one week a year when there's a sensational spring-clean. We have one in the house so why not across the whole country? You could save the money spent on street cleaning and spend it on re-cycling schemes'

Taraq, 30

JANE TEWSON

Money is not the only way of giving. If we really want to live in a more cohesive society, we must start giving of our time, our talents and our skills

'To feel depressed, cheated, bitter, desperate, vulnerable, frightened, angry, worried about debts or job and housing insecurity; to feel devalued, useless, helpless, uncared for, hopeless, isolated, anxious and a failure: these feelings can dominate people's whole experience of life.'

(Richard Wilkinson, Unhealthy Societies, Routledge, 1996)

I have two visions of our communities in the early decades of the new Millennium.

In the first, I see division – thickening walls of silence, disengagement and mistrust – between people of different cultures, between the 'haves' and the 'have-nots', between neighbours who never quite manage to reach out and talk. A privatised world, where people suffer and celebrate behind closed doors. Where people are more likely to feel involved in *EastEnders* than in their own neighbourhood, to 'interface' in 'virtual communities' than to talk to the person next door.

In the second vision of the future, I see connection – vital links of shared experience, understanding and mutual support – between people from all backgrounds. People reaching out across every divide and over every doorstep to share their stories and their talents, confident that everyone has something to give, and unashamed to admit that each of us needs support at some point in our lives.

I would like to believe that, collectively, we can use the unique momentum of the Millennium to begin to make the second vision real. The turning of this Millennium, this once-in-40-generations experience, must be the time to dream big dreams and, more importantly, to put in the sort of sustained effort which will bring them to life. Imagine if all 58 million of us in the UK decided that from now on we would regularly reach out to make a practical difference in our neighbourhoods. Over time, this could bring about a sea-change in our culture and a total revitalisation of our communities.

Over the last year, Pilotlight (a small, maverick charity which I founded two years ago), has brought together people from different professions and walks of life to try and imagine the power that could be generated by that collective 'reaching out', and what it would take to set it alight. David Robinson and his team at Community Links have been a crucial guide and inspiration in this process. What Community Links makes happen across Newham, giving people the confidence and tools not just to get help, but to give it, has grounded our vision at every step, and given us faith that it can work.

We have called our idea ONE20. Perhaps that could be a date – 1/1/2000. Perhaps it could be one 20th of everybody's working week, dedicated to involvement in the community. Or one person's skill and passion multiplied 20 times. Or 20 years in which to change the world. Our hope is that people will take part, and then tell *us* what it means!

ONE20 is a vision, a catalyst and 'toolkit' to help inspire and enable everyone – from stressed-out City traders to isolated older people and unemployed 17-year-olds – to give their time, passion and skill in their local neighbourhood, and transform their own sense of community and achievement along the way.

Of course, this happens already. Many people are involved in volunteering schemes: they go shopping for a neighbour, or look after someone else's kids during a family crisis. But where is this culture of sharing – of reaching out to make a difference to one-self and others – encouraged and celebrated on a grand scale? Where is it systematically supported by business and government?

10

Where is it seen as normal and fun? Where do ordinary people go to find the motivation to become involved, or inspiring examples of what can be done, or accessible information about where their skills are needed locally?

Our dream is that ONE20 will become a catalyst for all of this activity. If it succeeds, we hope it will help to build a more inclusive society, where pride is based on communal as much as individual achievement, and in which people give time in their communities as a matter of course.

Achieving this vision is an enormous task. And we are determined not to spawn another enormous bureaucracy to make it happen. Instead we want to help kick-start an unstoppable movement which, ultimately, is owned and run by everyone, from the bottom up. ONE20's role will be to inspire people – from those in big organisations to individuals – to get involved, to make it easy for them to do their bit, and to tap into the wealth of knowledge and activity that's already out there in communities.

Coming up with the practical steps to encourage such a sea-change in society has really challenged us. What has helped most is to remember that the ancient traditions are usually the best. What have people always done when they have wanted to build cohesion in their communities? They have told stories, had big celebrations, and exchanged ideas and information. This, essentially, is what ONE20 will be doing – but we'll be doing it with 21st-century tools. Using television to tell the human stories behind burning social issues, and to celebrate what people are already doing to turn their communities around. Using the latest publishing technology to produce a 'rough guide' to giving time in your locality, to be dropped on everyone's doorstep. And setting up telephone call-centres so that people can easily access information about how to get involved. The trick will be to take advantage of these new technologies, put them to use in making us feel connected, and in touch with each other – rather than allowing them to distance us from what's happening outside our front doors, as so often happens now.

Another essential part of any traditional community event is the full and active participation of the community's leaders. Again, we want ONE20 to reinterpret the tradition, and bring it up to date. As well as challenging politicians, chief executives of big companies, media stars, or the editors of local papers to roll up their sleeves and get involved, ONE20 will be tracking down the 'unsung heroes' who make every community tick. We will give them the chance to make their voices heard, and ask them to pass on ideas which they believe can bring about meaningful change.

There is one major tradition, though, that ONE20 wants to totally reinvent and reinvigorate – even turn on its head. This is the now accepted belief that 'charity' and 'philanthropy' are mainly about money – specifically, those who have it giving to those who don't.

Of course, money is crucial, and desperately needed. But too often giving money, rather than connecting us with each other, simply puts barriers between us, ultimately disempowering both the giver and the receiver. Handing over £1 to a person living on the street might stop us feeling guilty, and buy them a coffee, but it can also prevent us from having a conversation which could ultimately benefit both parties. In this way, social engagement can become just another transaction in the market-place. And those who don't have any money are prevented from contributing at all.

By focusing on people getting directly involved and giving of themselves – their time, talents and skills – ONE20 will seek to open up a whole new approach to 'charity'. One which is inclusive, direct and mutual, and which actively embraces human connection as a vital part of social change. Restoring people's confidence – whatever part of the social spectrum they occupy – that they in themselves have something to contribute, something to share that will make a difference, is perhaps ONE20's most important aim.

One of the major barriers to achieving that aim is the very language we use to describe social issues. This has got to change. To be labelled as 'socially excluded', to be told you attend a 'failing school' or live on a 'sink estate' is an instant silencer, blocking your potential and initiative. Even words like 'community' (which I have used so liberally here) can backfire for people who feel that it's precisely 'the community' that is shutting them out.

The only way to change that language is to change the mindset behind it. It's exactly the same mindset which tells us that 'they' (the marginalised, the excluded ones) need 'us' (the mainstream, the privileged) to bestow solutions to their problems from above. By bringing people face to face to tackle problems which affect us all, we hope ONE20 will begin to turn such prejudice around. The truth is that it's people who have been through the mill themselves who often have the most to contribute, and the best ideas for workable solutions.

This is why, in building the vision of ONE20, we have tried to stay close to the work and spirit of grassroots organisations like Community Links. It is here that we've tapped into the real inspiration and ideas. On a recent visit, a small number of us spent time with a group of Asian women who had come together to tackle domestic violence. I was moved to ask the one thing that would make the most difference in their lives. 'Breaking the silence about what is happening,' they said. Breaking that silence, finding powerful and authentic ways to tell the truth about hidden problems in our communities and matching them with inspiring examples of how people, like those Asian women, are working together to confront them – has now become a central aim of ONE20's media strategy.

Everyone who has worked on ONE20, I think, has shared with me an overwhelming sense that what we are hoping to achieve is at one and the same time crazy and unrealistic and totally necessary. (Perhaps this is how all of us feel in confronting the enormous needs and the enormous potential ahead of us in the new Millennium.)

But I hope it isn't only blind faith that keeps us going, and makes us believe that something as ambitious as ONE20 could actually work. I really don't think so. I believe all of us know, because we feel it ourselves and see it all around us, that there is a very real hunger in our society for reconnection and re-engagement. And it's often the darkest moments that tell us it is there. In response to atrocious tragedies on the news. When we walk past – or even step over – people living on the street.

Faith does come into it, though. We have to have faith in the fact that it is the very depth of our despair and frustration that will turn us around – if only we are grabbed by the collar and shown what to do. We have to believe that the moment when old traditions and language are wearing out is the very moment that is ripe for re-invention. It is that sort of moment, I hope, that we all lived through at the stroke of midnight on 31 December 1999. I just hope we can grab its potential by the tail.

Tell me. I forget.
Show me. I remember.
Involve me. I understand.

Jane Tewson was the founder of Charity Projects and the co-founder of Comic Relief. She is now director of Pilotlight, a small charity which seeks to act as a catalyst for adventurous approaches to social change

'I'm a do-er but I need support to stop me asking why I am bothering, I'd like to know a champion inside the council who I could go to for some help, someone who I know would fight our corner'

Jo, 65

Number 11

Revving Up the Voluntary Sector

DANIEL SILVERSTONE

Today's voluntary organisations are at best innovative, iconoclastic and inspiring, at worst parochial, plodding and unrepresentative. What changes should be made to help them meet the challenges of the 21st century?

At the start of this century charities in the UK could have looked back with some pride on the previous 100 years – a century in which they had carried out pioneering roles as:

- the precursors of state services – schools, hospitals
- service providers of last resort – childcare, soup kitchens
- advocates for change – in public policy, by establishing minimum thresholds
- advocates on behalf of deprived and marginalised groups – the working poor, immigrants
- the founders of many pathfinder services - i.e. services too 'dangerous' for the state or the churches to embrace: family planning, civil rights, and so on.

A similar scan of the present century would produce a rather more muddled and complex picture. Among today's non-profit-making organisations, there are thousands of individual players, all searching for distinctive roles and voices and all seeking their own definable space amid the switchback rides of this century's public policy – minimum protection, two world wars, strong state, welfarism, weak state, safety-net, producer-led economy, consumer-led economy, contracting public services, the decline of active citizenship, globalisation, regionalisation. The list goes on.

Looking ahead to the start of the new century, where does what is now described as the voluntary sector stand? What is its definable space? What should be its unique contributions to the next Millennium?

I believe the case needs to be re-made for the voluntary

sector's contribution in the 21st century. And, to this end, I have identified six overlapping areas of change. Before embarking on this star-gazing, though, I would like to offer my own assessment of the current state of play vis-à-vis non-profit-making activity with the following brief and, I accept, provocative typology.

The voluntary sector on the threshold of the new Millennium is:

AT BEST	AT WORST
unbureaucratic	inward-looking
innovative	searching for a halcyon era
iconoclastic	parochial
voice for the voiceless	unrepresentative
front-runner for tomorrow's services	outmoded services
inspiring	plodding
high public esteem, trust	overlooked, unnoticed
charismatic leaders	very charismatic leaders

So much for the voluntary sector itself. What about the public policy environment, from which voluntary organisations are increasingly going to have to take their lead? The buzz-words of public policy on the cusp of the Millennium are: pragmatic; non-ideological; inclusive; accountable; transparent; joined-up; defining outcomes; auditing effectiveness; heterogeneous; no single models; regional; European and global.

Both listings are offered with tremulousness but with, I believe, a degree of fin-de-siècle realism. Taken together, they make the process of star-gazing, on which I shall now embark, somewhat less uncertain.

There are, as I say, six areas where I believe non-profit-making players can confidently mark out some niche terrain in the early years of the new century.

1. Out-of-sector Activity

Non-profit-making players need to avoid becoming trapped within the increasingly narrow confines of the voluntary sector – a categorisation which potentially covers billion-pound housing associations, the burgeoning ethical business sector within the social economy and the Royal National Institute for the Blind, as well as single-employee refugee organisations and all-volunteer neighbourhood watch schemes.

With the boundaries between public and private, national and transnational becoming less and less clear, the niche imperative for voluntary players lies in:

a) developing out-of-sector partnerships within the 'voluntary sector': e.g. homeless agencies organising for street sleepers to attend courses in theatrical stage management; refugee org-anisations offering translation services to housing associations.

b) developing cutting-edge models that can be applied and modified elsewhere in the UK and worldwide (the *Big Issue*, hospices), or in different sectors altogether (e.g. old peoples' homes inviting in voluntary sector practitioners to provide age reminiscence courses for their residents).

c) the forming of sustainable alliances between major companies and individual organisations (e.g. Tate & Lyle and Community Links), with the relationships extending way beyond money.

2. Demythologising the Voluntary Sector

The entrenched set of images that the public associates with the 'voluntary sector' will be difficult to dislodge. The Government itself locates the 'voluntary sector' within a department of the

Home Office, which is primarily responsible for prisons, police, immigration and criminal justice. The recent temporary sojourn of responsibility for the sector within the Department for Culture was apocryphally explained, by an anonymous mandarin, as 'something people do in their spare time'. In the future we must undertake a radical rethink of how UK institutions and opinion-formers define, describe and see the voluntary sector. There will be huge opportunities for the sector to redefine itself, without, hopefully, unnecessarily sacrificing its core defining features. Rapid changes in language and cultural expectations will be called for.

3. Future Generations of Community Leaders
Non-profit-making organisations have always provided a con-veyor-belt for future community leaders – locally, regionally and nationally. And, as the public has increasingly lost trust in the institutions which have navigated most of the present century, non-profit-making players will have important cards to play to enhance their own influence and profile. That said, they will need to steer a careful path between becoming indistin-guishable from tarnished mainstream institutions (some giant housing associations come to mind here) and clinging to out-moded, isolating approaches. If this route is well-navigated, sub-stantial and long-term community leadership opportunities will emerge, with the voluntary sector uniquely positioned to benefit.

4. Social Inclusion
The voluntary sector may bow its head at the shrine of equality, rights and diversity but its performance has been decidedly patchy – particularly with regard to its employment responsibilities. How many black voluntary sector chief executives can you name? In my judgment, voluntary sector performance in this key area lags considerably behind many local and health

authorities, some government departments and an increasing number of private sector employers. If the voluntary sector is to continue to burnish many of its core images – caring, fair, supportive to the underdog – it must take active steps to more accurately reflect the communities and interests it claims to serve.

5. Niche Positioning

Within the context of a permanently changing, unpredictable environment, non-profit-making players will need to concentrate as never before on niche positioning. This will require careful and continuous review and finely judged and regular assessments of the balance between an organisation's core founding principles on the one hand, and the changing patterns of public policy and the means by which these policies are going to be delivered, on the other.

a) Pathways out of social exclusion

Over the last 10 years European policy discourse has seen familiar terms, such as 'poverty', 'disadvantage' and 'deprivation', give way to that of 'social exclusion'. The broad aim of creating a socially *inclusive* society is increasingly influenced by a recognition of the growing institutional and generation gaps in income, life chances, education, health and discrimination. At its best the voluntary sector is uniquely placed to advocate on behalf of socially excluded people and communities; to act as a trusted intermediary and as a linking agency between government and (potentially) corporate players and the most excluded groups in UK society; and to become the most appropriate deliverer of services to these groups.

b) Representation

Citizenship, lobbying, democratic representation, voting... all of these key civic issues are under enormous strain as we enter the new Millennium. The continuous revolution in new technology will inevitably open up further areas of direct contact, engagement and influence. And the voluntary sector is well positioned to directly represent views and ideas within the developing civic landscape – regional government, citizens' juries, city mayors, etc.

c) Risk

I have already referred to those many public services which are today regarded as mainstream or universal in such areas as public health, education and childcare, which were originally pioneered within the voluntary sector. Inevitably, at the outset, such ideas and services were considered risky, even off-message, insane and dangerous. The voluntary sector needs to concentrate on developing its niche position as a laboratory for new thinking and practice. Funding agencies (see below) need to rise to the challenge of becoming less risk-averse; to support potentially beneficial high-risk proposals; and to recognise that some, maybe all of their investment will be lost, and yet be willing, following private sector practice, to accept a degree of loss set against the clear benefits that will accrue as some high-risk models break through to the mainstream.

6. Joined-Up Funding

Voluntary organisations are totally dependent on an increasingly complex mix of funding – contracts, charitable giving and earned income. Funders of all types have a moral public policy and business-led responsibility to deliver funding strategies which are more effective and sustainable, less bureaucratic, which encourage initiative and innovation and which are specifically geared to supporting pathways out of social exclusion. There are a number of encouraging signs, as I write, that many funders are beginning to see the benefits of 'joined-up' funding. Positive developments in this area should include:

- Joining up funders and fundseekers – breaking down the

artificial barriers between the two. In the United States, regional associations of 'grant-makers' regularly brief fund-seekers on how successfully to bid for their funding and hold round-table events on particular issues – homelessness, venture capital, early reading schemes and so on. Applying this model to the developing regional environment within the UK would deliver quick dividends.

■ Sharing information, monitoring and evaluation. Funders need to be better informed, less wasteful and less bureaucratic. They need to share critical data more effectively. At present the London Funders' Group, a cross-sectoral network of 100 funders with an aggregate spend exceeding £400 million, which I chair, is concluding a major 'single application form' project. Assuming that a critical mass of funders adopt or adapt this form, we will be able drastically to reduce levels of bureaucracy and transaction costs both for fund-seekers and funders and to greatly increase the sharing of key information between funders.

■ The continuum of risk. I have already commented on risk, and believe that funders have a key complementary role to play, with fund-seekers, in managing issues of risk more effectively. At regional, national and (potentially) EU level, funders should be encouraged to consider what level of risk they are prepared to undertake.

In today's funding environment, charitable trusts tend to be open to high-risk funding; corporate funders mainly cluster around the medium-risk range – they are open to innovative ideas but want some guarantees of a return; while national and local government funders, in thrall to the Treasury or local auditors, traditionally congregate at the low-risk end of the spectrum. By improving the collective understanding of where individual funders fit on the risk continuum, funders will quickly improve their capacity to package multi-funded arrangements where the funding burden passes down the risk continuum from high to low in stages as the project moves through its lifespan.

■ Two-way learning. Traditionally, funders monitor fund-seekers, not vice versa. But in practice, funders may have much to learn from fund-seekers. There may well be organisational, cultural, customer-related and service areas where the cutting practice of particular voluntary organisations could provide instructive and helpful models for government and local government, health bodies, corporate donors, family trusts, and so on. Quality assurance systems and tools need to be developed for the new Millennium which will encourage and deliver this sort of two-way learning. Such a step, while clearly beneficial in itself, will also .significantly improve the quality and sustainability of partnerships between non-profit-making players and the other key sectors within UK society.

Daniel Silverstone is the director of London Boroughs Grants, an organisation funded by the 33 London boroughs, which provides a substantial grants programme in support of voluntary action in London

'The cause of disability does not lie within the individual but within the way society is organised. It's the way society treats me that makes me disabled. We need to change society at all levels starting with the new generation. I want people to see what I *can* do and not what I *can't* do'

Michelle, 25

STEVE HILTON

In the new Millennium businesses need to rediscover their social conscience, to recognise that they are involved in *shaping* society, not just *selling* to it

Tony Blair is seething. The famous grin has disappeared, along with all the jobs at the Siemens factory in his constituency. It doesn't matter that he runs the country. It doesn't matter that the factory was set up, just after the election, with hefty financial support from the Government. Siemens says it must close. Nothing the Prime Minister can do.

Bill Gates is fuming. The more successful he is, the more he is hated. He creates jobs, and wealth and millionaires – yet he's branded an ogre. He gives billions to charity, and receives scorn in return. What's he to do, lose money? Go bust? How would that help anyone?

David Robinson, the director of Community Links, is sighing. His East End charity's gone from strength to strength, after 21 years of passionate work. He's got blue-chip supporters, hefty donations, great volunteers. But still he sees a depressing picture, in which business puts its social conscience in a box marked 'charity', but most of the time utterly ignores the issues that that box raises.

What is going on? Three different people, three different sectors, three different frustrations. Politicians are frustrated because the world of big business seems to be usurping their power. Businesses are frustrated because the world is expecting more of them in areas they know little about. Charities are frustrated because their world seems to be as marginalised as ever, while the issues they deal with are somehow more intractable than before. And in the middle of all this are the people on the receiving end of these three sectors: voters, customers, charity 'users'. Very often they are the same people, and they are frustrated too. They can see what needs to be done in the world, but aren't as clear as they used to be about whose job it is to do it.

Politics, business, charity. As we move into the new Millennium, the relationships between these sectors are excitingly fluid, with huge opportunities for us to make them work better, to everyone's benefit. But if that is going to happen, they need to be clear about their respective roles. I'm going to concentrate on business. The early industrialists were very clear about their social role. They knew that their business success depended on productive workers. Workers who lived without adequate food, shelter and education were not productive. So in the absence of a welfare state, the leaders of the first great companies stepped in to provide meals, homes and classrooms for their workers and their families. It was a case of enlightened self-interest: 'I look after you, you work hard for me.' And, in this sense, the Rowntrees and Rockefellers were not just businessmen. They saw themselves as agents for the good, part of the system, a force in the land.

Go to Rockefeller Plaza in New York City, and you'll see what I mean. Stand directly opposite the GE building, the tallest skyscraper. If you've ever seen a photo of festive New Yorkers ice-skating in the open air, it will have been taken from here. But look down for a second. In front of you is a bronze plaque. On it are inscribed the words of Joseph D Rockefeller. A businessman. This is what he had to say:

I believe in the supreme worth of the individual and his right to life, liberty and the pursuit of happiness.

I believe that every right implies a responsibility; every opportunity, an obligation; every possession, a duty.

I believe that the law was made for man and not man for the law; that government is the servant of the people and not their master.

I believe in the dignity of labour, whether with head or hand; that the world owes no man a living, but that it owes every man an opportunity to make a living.

I believe that thrift is essential to well ordered living and that economy is a prime requisite of a sound financial structure, whether in government, business or personal affairs.

I believe that truth and justice are fundamental to an enduring social order.

I believe in the sacredness of a promise, that a man's word should be as good as his bond; that character - not wealth or power or position - is of supreme worth.

I believe that the rendering of useful service is the common duty of mankind and that only in the purifying fire of sacrifice is the dross of selfishness consumed and the greatness of the human soul set free.

I believe in an all-wise and all-loving god, named by whatever name, and that the individual's highest fulfilment, greatest happiness and widest usefulness are to be found in living in harmony with his will.

I believe that love is the greatest thing in the world; that it alone can overcome hate; that right can and will triumph over might.'

These are amazing words. Whether you consider them to be the self-indulgent pontifications of a pompous egomaniac, or the poetic declarations of a passionate visionary, you've got to admit that it's hard to imagine today's business leaders speaking in these terms. Certainly they are not words which would fit comfortably alongside the bland mission statements that litter the reception areas of the modern corporate world. However much you paid them, I don't suppose the management consultants would come up with this kind of stuff.

Rockefeller, though, hailed from a different age: his words show that, for him anyway, there was no distinction between making money and making the world a better place: it was all part of the same 'project', as we've now learned to call these things. Back then, civic duty mattered as much as share-holder value.

Another great business figure once expressed a similar view in a more direct and less overblown manner. Think of those occasions when your boss has addressed you and your fellow workers together – perhaps at a Christmas party, or an annual get-together. Have you ever heard anything like this?

'I want to discuss why a company exists in the first place. In other words, why are we here? I think that many people wrongly assume that a company exists to make money. While this is an important result of a company's activities, we have to go deeper to find the real reasons for being. As we investigate this, we inevitably come to the conclusion that a group of people get together to exist as an institution that we call a company so that they are able to accomplish something together that they would not be able to accomplish separately – they make a contribution to society, a phrase which sounds trite, but is fundamental.'

That was Dave Packard, founder of Hewlett-Packard, speaking to a group of his staff around 40 years ago. Of course it's easy to knock it as pious rubbish – the sort that simply forms one stage in the classic life-cycle of a successful businessman. You know the story from a hundred profiles in the financial pages: invent money-making scheme at the age of 12; don't go to university; get job in huge industrial conglomerate; challenge decisions of dunderhead middle managers; get rebuffed; bump into chairman in lift; reveal plan for huge cost savings; become chief executive; become 'hatchet-man'; become 'nice'; do good works; write philosophical memoir; become head of arts/charity/sporting organisation; retire to mansion. In other words, the richer you become as an individual, the more you go on about 'society'. You can see this traditional model at work today – each survey of corporate philanthropy reveals new recruits to the army of do-gooders, more billions chucked in the charity box. The 1999 *US Chronicle of Philanthropy*'s charity donation league table records Bill Gates heading the list at $17 billion, followed by the Packard Foundation at $13 billion, and the Ford Foundation at over $11 billion.

I guess these business benefactors think they're being generous, decent and kind. In a sense they are. However cynically you choose to view their motives, you can't pretend that they don't give away significant stacks of cash. But the truth is, the amount of money that these businesses give to charity – whether corporately or through individual donations – is a pittance when measured against the financial size of the businesses themselves.

So let's go back to Dave Packard. I don't think his words about a 'contribution to society' are pious rubbish. I love his words, because they reveal a grasp of the true potential for business to do good. Not by giving away half a per cent of pre-tax profits to charity, but by seeing that a company's social contribution can and should be deeply entrenched in the everyday life of the business: in the products and services it sells, in the way it manufactures, in the way it treats its employees and suppliers, in the way it advertises, and in how it behaves in the community. Seen in these terms, social responsibility is not some kind of luxury for successful businesses, but a key to their success. The motivation for a business to think and act in this way should not be altruism, or philanthropy – but profit, because profit is the necessary fuel to finance a company's mission.

Dave Packard may have seen things this way, but soon after he made his mission statement the idea of making a 'contribution to society' fell out of fashion in business circles. Missionary industrialists were gradually replaced by corporations owned by share-holders. Value, not values, became the order of the day. As welfare states were established, more of the burdens of social responsibility were assumed by the state.

Thus the public sector was born and bred – a new force for good which would feed the hungry, house the homeless and teach children. All paid for through higher taxes, all delivered through the increasingly complex machinery of government. All-powerful, all-embracing. In this new world, people trusted the institutions of government to look after them. And in many ways, governments did: the growth of public education and health, social insurance, and countless other developments are testament to that.

But now look what's happened. As the century closes, the pendulum swings. Governments are fearful of taxing us, so they don't have the money they need to deliver their promises. The more they break their promises, the less we trust them. So governments have less and less power to do the things they want to do.

Business, meanwhile, is gaining more and more power. As a result of privatisation and deregulation, companies are now supplying services that used to be delivered by the state. Through marketing and communications, they've created brand names that we trust more than many of the old-established state institutions. And through liberalised financial markets, businesses are becoming global players on a scale that often puts the public sector in the shade. That's why Tony Blair was seething.

Unlike the early industrialists, though, today's companies are not led by social crusaders. They are led by business people, pure and simple. These people tend not to focus on their company's 'contribution to society' – why should they? It's not their job, not how their performance is measured.

This is what we need to change in the new Millennium. Business shouldn't stop being business-like when it comes to social issues. Quite the reverse: it's precisely by applying business skills to social challenges that the greatest progress is likely to be made. At the same time, companies, by seeing their social contribution as part of everyday business practice, will themselves benefit commercially. If you know that your customers care about education, why not use your regular contact with them, and the power of your brand, to help? Encourage parents to read with their children. Encourage your staff to be reading mentors. Help your customers provide equipment for schools.

It's true that much of this goes on already. Open any annual report, visit any corporate website, and you'll find words on social responsibility, community involvement, that sort of thing. These words will describe any number of excellent projects. But it's still seen as separate. It's not seen as *part* of the business, whatever the rhetoric says.

Too often, companies feel threatened when social issues are raised, and retreat into the arms of Lady Charity – 'If you want to know about our social commitments, look at our corporate giving.' But this completely misses the point. Such businesses fail to recognise the power they have, and they fail to exploit the opportunities this brings. I'll show you what I mean with a little case study from the US.

Aetna is one of America's largest insurance companies. A few years ago, it ran a campaign which, albeit on a small scale, encapsulates everything I've argued for. Rather than describe the campaign in great detail, I'll just reproduce the words of the advertisement that accompanied it:

**Every year, drunk drivers cost Aetna's
policy-holders at least $100 million.**

**Video cameras in police cars help
detect and deter drunk drivers.**

**We gave 10,000 video cameras to
police departments last year.**

**Aetna's policy-holders save money.
People don't die.**

Aetna. A policy to do more.

The beauty of this initiative is the clarity with which social and commercial objectives are aligned. There's no 'them and us', just a simple story which says: by helping out with a social issue, we benefit as a business, you benefit as customers, and we all benefit in our local communities. If Aetna can do it in America, don't tell me that businesses can't do it over here. They just need the confidence to go out on a limb, to state with conviction that they're involved in shaping society, not just selling to it.

If the business community is reticent, government and charities are in many ways ahead of corporate thinking in this area – perhaps because they need business so badly. The Prime Minister gave a clear endorsement of this approach not so long ago when he said: 'The 21st-century company will be different. Many of Britain's leading businesses are recognising that every customer is part of a community, and that social responsibility is not an optional extra.'

For a political leader to acknowledge – and indeed encourage – the participation of business in addressing the social issues his Government was elected to face, is a huge development, and one that must be sustained.

So, in the new Millennium, we need to *socialise* the commercial sector, and we need to *commercialise* the social sector. They'd both benefit, and government, business and charities would all find themselves helping to meet each others' goals, rather than worrying about why the goal-posts are moving.

Each of the sectors should do the things they do best, and each maximise its contribution to society. As each plays its part, each will gain its reward. Tony Blair, Bill Gates, David Robinson: in the years ahead, you could all be smiling.

Steve Hilton is a partner of Good Business, a social marketing consultancy

'If my benefit payments were paid over longer time frames, this would ease my cash flow problems and allow me to plan better'

Kathryn, 27

Number 13

Beyond the Poverty Trap

DAVID ROBINSON

Abolishing child poverty in 20 years? That, truly, is a Millennium vision

I think of Amir with sadness and guilt. He was the first and, at that time, the only Asian boy in my class. There were several Afro-Caribbean children, more than half the class was Jewish, but Amir was different and relentlessly bullied. At 12, I ran with the crowd. Merciless. The other children's friendship was not important to me; at school you were either protected on the inside or exposed on the outside. And on the outside life was hell.

All this came back to me last July as I listened to Gordon Brown talk about his plans for abolishing child poverty over the next 20 years. He was addressing a high-profile seminar of policy experts at Downing Street. And, when he set out the 20-year target and told the seminar, 'Be radical without being credible and credible without being radical – we aim to be both,' I was reminded of a lengthy, rather more private meeting that had occurred in the same room a fortnight before.

A group of six people had been invited through Community Links to come and share their experience of poverty with the Chancellor and discuss with him policies that could change their lives. I remembered the things we had talked about during that thoughtful, private meeting and I *believed*. One million children *will* be lifted out of poverty by April 2000, three million to go. Truly, a Millennium vision.

During the same period last summer, the *Guardian* published its 1999 survey of top directors' pay, revealing average increases of more than 26 per cent, five times the growth of average earnings and ten times the rate of inflation. A couple of days later, as I stood at the bus-stop outside Newham General Hospital, I listened to a conversation between two hospital workers, in which these directors' salaries were compared with those of a nurse, a surgeon and then an entire shift in the intensive care unit; you could throw in the Minister of Health, even the Prime Minister... the combined salaries of all these people still wouldn't top the salary of a single director with the key to the safe.

Harold Laski told a previous Labour government that you cannot tackle the problem of poverty without also tackling the problem of wealth. The Government is trying to do so – minimum wage, big increases in child benefit and income support for children under 11, Working Family Tax Credit, extra support for the poorest pensioners, etc. We can have it all, apparently. Eliminate poverty for the poor without sacrifice from the rest.

I am no economist but I know what kind of society I want for my children. A society without destitution – and anyone who believes we've got that already should spend a day at a Community Links advice session, visit our clothes bank or attend a play scheme. I want a society that sets a minimum standard of living, as six western nations have already done in the last ten years. More than that, a society that acknowledges the obscenity as well as the absurdity of huge differentials.

And that's why I remembered Amir that warm and optimistic morning in Downing Street last summer. Previous governments had talked about action for the poor but have only done things for the rich. This Government was demonstrating a commitment to tackling poverty, not just through the tax and benefit system but through Sure Start, New Deal and other major programmes.

Still, I just thought of Amir: I remembered hanging back and walking home with him, helping him with his homework, even giving him money. All this, always, when the other kids were not around. In company, on the contrary, I talked the tyrants' talk – insulting, undermining, threatening. What sense of worth did Amir take out into the world when he was eventually free of us? Even then I knew that doing things by stealth wasn't enough. It was

13

timid, the recourse of a follower not a leader.

I think of Amir and the bullies I never reached. I think of the Community Links families and the Chancellor in the sunny room.

In company, I would talk the tyrants' ta

I think of the top earners in the clover, and I want for the new Millennium:

1. An open debate engaging us all.

Inequality is not just an issue for the poor. Richard Wilkinson, in his book *Unhealthy Societies* (Routledge,1996), has shown, first, that increases in social cohesion are largely dependent on reducing the size of income differences; second, that smaller differentials and increased social cohesion play an important role in reducing national death rates; and third, that in modern economies narrower income differences are associated with faster economic growth. Perhaps a Commission on Remuneration in the UK could highlight these issues, debate the ethical questions, publicise the facts and suggest a moral base for making judgments about remuneration in this new Millennium. Commission members could be drawn from across society and the link with the Millennium would be a deliberate attempt both to depersonalise and depoliticise the process. It wouldn't be about your salary and

insulting, undermining, threatening...

mine, here and now, but about the kind of society we want for our children and our children's children.

I have led Community Links for 21 years and received enormous support from business leaders. I am proud to count many not only as supporters but as friends. Our bank manager may worry that I am turning to savage the hand that has fed us. Those same friends will not. Respected leaders establish and consistently articulate a clear personal moral code. Day after day we cope with the consequences of poverty and we struggle with the causes. Little would have been achieved without the resources of our friends but much much more has yet to be done. We are all of the real world. We do what can be done, in our respective positions, here and now, and we wrestle with the moral dilemmas. As Jesse Jackson would say, 'God hasn't finished with any of us yet.'

13

2. A society that recognises not only the importance of money but also its limitations.

A couple of weeks ago I came across a prosperous family which would, in the current jargon, be considered to be at least as 'dysfunctional' as any in our poorest communities. I noticed that the 11-year-old boy had, among other things, a pristine Liverpool strip, but apparently neither friends nor family to play with. He may become a lawyer as his father expects. I think it is equally likely that he will be sleeping in Temple Gardens by the time he is 20. 'You cannot,' as Elizabeth Fry noted, 'give a child love by act of parliament.' We all need help at some time in our lives and we all have something to give, not top down, rich to poor, but two-way, for mutual fulfilment. Each of us has, like supporters of the American Civil Rights Movement, 'the power of one'. How many of us use it?

3. A state that really embraces the talents, the experience, the creativity and the energy of the many.

It is difficult to overstate the siege mentality that has grown up among many good people working in our inner-city schools, social service departments, hospitals and community agencies. Simply getting through the day, avoiding risks, keeping in touch with the league tables – these have become the extent of the vision. We need to raise people's sights and we need to do it from the top. We need to say that it is fine to take risks and we need to recognise that some risks will fail. Above all, we need to acknowledge that we share responsibility for the next generation and we all have a part to play.

4. Leadership that connects poverty and wealth, talking and doing, government and people.

Lao Tsu wrote: 'The wicked leader is he whom the people despise.

The good leader is he whom the people revere. The great leader is he whose people say, "We did it ourselves."' If we, the Millennium generation, can say in 20 years' time, 'We abolished poverty,' we will truly have experienced the leadership we deserve.

David Robinson is the director of Community Links

'When I was young, they got people doing community service to clear up the slag-heap next to East Ham Park. Why can't we get people doing community service or people in prison working on big projects for the good of the community?'

Henry, 52

Number 14
In Search of Community UK plc

DAVID GRAYSON

What if businesses *really* worked with community groups? What if they were convinced that they could benefit from forming long-term partnerships with organisations like Community Links?

Imagine a day in the life of an organisation like Community Links – let's call it Can-Do – in the not-too-distant future. Can-Do is a Trust which serves a tough, inner-city neighbourhood, and runs a range of facilities for children, teenagers, parents, pensioners and disabled people. There are art workshops, English-as-a-foreign-language classes; a benefits advice service; counselling groups; a toy library and a café.

Can-Do's flagship activity, though, is its new **'Learning for Life'** centre, aimed at people of all ages who want to take on some form of education at their own pace, using a range of media – CD ROMs, the Internet, and so on. The 'Learning for Life' centre is a **social franchise,** part of a national network for which the organisation has the local licence (having found that it was easier and more effective to take on an established franchise, than to try and invent a similar programme from scratch).

This morning, Janet, the co-director of Can-Do, is preparing for the next board meeting of one of the major banks – of which she has recently become a director (she remains the only **community entrepreneur** on the board, but the bank is considering taking on another one).

In the conference room, her co-director, John, is busy preparing for the annual **'Ten(d) to Zero'** meeting with the Trust's main corporate partner. Every year the two organisations sit down together and evaluate each key aspect of their partnership: 'aspects which are very poor score a 10. Those which are excellent score a zero – hence the objective to move from 'Ten(d) to zero'.

Upstairs, a group of volunteers are undergoing **staff coaching** in **mentoring skills** for a new outreach programme with at-risk teenagers. One volunteer, Guy – a young corporate financier – is plugged in via an Internet chat room, having had to go off to see a key corporate client in Frankfurt unexpectedly the night before. Another, Jill, has been acting as an **'absentee volunteer'** over the Internet for the last six months, ever since her law firm transferred her to the Shanghai office.

After lunch, a project team of **volunteers and paid staff** meet to discuss the results of the latest **social audit** which the Trust has undertaken – and, in particular, how well they are communicating the work and services of the Trust to their different stakeholders.

Later, the board of the Trust grab an hour to watch a long-awaited programme on the **Community Television Channel.**

And finally, last thing at night when most of the building has emptied, staff from another local voluntary organisation come in to make use of Can-Do's IT facilities – to **surf the Internet** and swop information and ideas with a fellow group of organisations working with HIV+ and Aids issues in California.

This vision of mutually beneficial partnership between a community group and the business sector may sound a bold one. But it is actually an increasingly realisable one. All the technological innovations I have described above are already available in Britain. One of the most exciting challenges now is to identify successful business expertise and models which can be sensitively and appropriately adapted for application in community organisations. Let me go through those cited in the vision above, piece by piece:

Learning for Life Centre

All of us, whatever our backgrounds and previous qualifications, are now going to have to get used to learning and re-learning throughout our lives. The problem which must be addressed, though, is how to make this learning and re-learning accessible to the 'getting nowhere' generation – and not just in conventional educational centres. Take the Cyberskills Workshop, first begun in Bristol and now being promoted by ICL across the country (and indeed internationally). These workshops can be very liberating, in terms of inter-generation contacts, and can overcome people's fear of the new information and communications technologies and be a gateway to a whole range of new learning opportunities.

Social franchise

The Cyberskills Workshop is effectively a social franchise. Community organisations are increasingly borrowing techniques like 'franchising' from business. Just as franchising has proved a safe halfway house for many people wanting to run their own businesses with the security of following a proven model, so now there are successful community programmes which can be 'franchised'. With a social franchise you get the best of both worlds – both the cafetière (top-down) and the percolator (bottom-up) approach to community regeneration.

Companies active in the community are frequently complaining that they are inundated with requests from community organisations to support their 'unique' project or programme, when actually theirs is very similar to many other projects that business is already supporting. Social franchises would cut down this problem; enable business and community to get 'more bangs for the bucks' and spread good practice further and faster. So if, for example, Lloyds TSB are supporting an innovative project to help people with learning disabilities in the North East, and it is successful, they might turn this into a social franchise. Then, when, say, Whitbread's get asked to support something similar in, for example, Portsmouth, they might – instead – help the Portsmouth group to become the local franchisee of the north-eastern organisation.

A Community Entrepreneur on the Board

Big companies are used to having non-executives from other companies, as well as academics and politicians, on their boards, but I don't know of a single FT100 company in the UK which has yet appointed someone from a community organisation as a board member. Undoubtedly, big companies are losing out here. The skills which voluntary organisations have are increasingly relevant to corporate boards – how to manage diversity, for example, or how to gain early warning of changes in social perceptions of business.

After Shell's Brent Spar and Nigeria debacles, Cor Herkstrotter, the then worldwide boss of Shell, concluded: 'We have to admit that we have made mistakes, we have not handled some of the new challenges as well as we could have... I am talking about a series of faulty assessments, misreadings of the situation which have led us to take poor management decisions... Why do they come about? I think that the fundamental answer lies in our failure to fully recognise the social and technological changes... Simply put, the institutions of global society are being reinvented, as technology redefines relations between individuals and organisations.'

Having access to different perspectives in the boardroom is going to become more and more important.

The 'Ten(d) to Zero' Model

Ten(d) to Zero is a system developed by the auto-parts firm, Unipart, as a means of monitoring its long-term relationships with suppliers. But it could just as easily be used between a community organisation and its business partner. Every voluntary organisation

14

should have at least one substantial, long-term, two-way relationship with a business. The Ten(d) to Zero type model is a way of making this sort of relationship work.

Volunteer Staff Coaching

Just as in business life nowadays employees expect regular opportunities to acquire new skills and update their learning (indeed having such opportunities is an important factor for many in choosing a job); so the best volunteers will expect to be able to undergo specialist training in the voluntary organisations they are working for, in order to have the most impact possible.

Mentoring skills

Mentoring is a valuable way of developing people's potential. Business in the Community (of which I am a director) has developed a series of mentoring programmes under which business people act as mentors (advisors, facilitators, inspirers) to trainees and potential new recruits. Our 'Roots and Wings' programme has been particularly targeted at 'at-risk' young people.

The Absentee Volunteer

If voluntary organisations are going to attract and retain the services of some of the burgeoning numbers of highly mobile 'global cosmopolitans' that now inhabit cities like London and New York, they are going to have to be able to respond to these people's lifestyles and work commitments. New York City Cares is one organisation which is particularly geared up for efficient communication with its network of New York volunteers. They run hour-long induction sessions – on three evenings per week. They also hold in-company orientation seminars and run an Internet site. Volunteers receive a monthly magazine, listing all volunteering opportunities each day with precise times and descriptions.

Additionally, there is a last-minute volunteering hotline which is updated once a week with volunteering opportunities that are still open for the following weekend. Because of the substantial investment they have made in IT, the staff at City Cares know which volunteer has done what and can generate thank-you notes for extra service. Business in the Community is now working with a group of companies, as well as the Home Office and several voluntary organisations, to adapt this concept for the UK under the umbrella of 'Cares Incorporated'.

Volunteers and Paid Staff
It is going to become increasingly difficult to tell these two apart. My friend Geoff makes his money as a masseur and as an aromatherapist, but when he goes into the offices of a campaigning organisation where he volunteers, he talks about 'going into work'.

Social Audits
In the future, voluntary organisations are going to have to deal with the same sort of increased scrutiny and pressure from vigilante consumers of their services as government and business have already had to face. A new generation of more articulate and assertive disabled people, for example, is demanding much greater control over organisations that serve disabled people: the move is from organisations *for* disabled people to organisations *of* disabled people. This is going to be a general trend – hence the new enthusiasm for social auditing. The New Economies Foundation – a leading pioneer of social audits – has developed an auditing methodology specifically adapted for non-profit-making organisations. I believe that companies and other supporters are increasingly going to want to know more about the effectiveness of prospective community partners, and the social audit is the ideal

way of gaining such knowledge. It could become part of a major company's standard 'due diligence' investigations. And maybe vice versa too.

Community TV Channel

Businesses and other organisations on both sides of the Atlantic are increasingly using dedicated business TV channels for two-way communication, training and briefings. The costs are plummeting. And now this business model is being adopted by the voluntary sector. The Media Trust, a British charity, is currently mobilising communications industry support for the establishment of a Community TV channel in Britain. This is a good example of a particular business sector being inspired to work on a specific community problem relevant to that industry. There are many other examples of this sort of partnership: the food retailing sector is now being encouraged to help transfer purchasing expertise, etc, to community-owned supermarkets; the utility companies are helping to form community mutual societies which can buy energy for their members more cheaply; and banks are supporting financial literacy programmes.

Surfing the Net

When I visited the original Cyberskills Workshop in Bristol, its organisers told me of a Women's Refuge in Swindon which had gone on the Internet and come across a similar centre in Seattle. The two organisations are now communicating regularly with each other, exchanging ideas and techniques.

So, what of all this? The benefits to community organisations of going into partnership with business are fairly clear. They stand to gain:

– **technical expertise**

- firepower/clout: the ability to open doors
- credibility: the possibility of being taken more seriously
- contacts
- an ability to focus on making things happen and to get results
- a better understanding of customer-focus
- financial discipline

As for the benefits to business, some of these are already widely accepted. Community involvement can build up and expand the skills of volunteer-employees, as well as the loyalty of the company's workforce generally; it can also boost a company's long-term corporate reputation and be an investment in the 'goodwill bank' among the stakeholders of the company. Working with particularly innovative groups like Community Links can help an entire business to learn new skills of networking and creative thinking.

But, if these sorts of partnership are really going to work, many community organisations are going to have be more pro-active and self-confident in asserting what they can contribute. Taskforce 2002 (sponsored by Business in the Community and the National Council of Voluntary Organisations), which a few years ago brought together leaders from large and small firms, together with representatives from national charities and frontline community groups, identified some of the benefits which non-profit-making players can offer business, such as early warning of society's concerns; 'innocence by association' (i.e gaining a share of the positive, worthy image which tends to be associated with voluntary organisations); and acquiring skills in motivating an increasingly mobile cosmopolitan workforce. In their report, published in 1998, Taskforce 2002 articulated a vision of a 'Two-way Street' – mutually beneficial relationships between business and non-profit-making players. We saw this as being healthier to both sides, far

14

more sustainable in tough times, and more replicable.

Creating and sustaining cross-sectoral partnerships is no easy task. It may come naturally to a few visionaries. Most of us, though, would benefit from learning from what has worked already. Why, for instance, have some communities had a long track record of good partnerships? What is in the air or the water in those areas? Are there some critical success factors like taking the time to build up trust between the partners, the time to develop a clear vision and strategy – with an agreed action plan to deliver definite accountabilities and timescales – and active communications to ensure that the wider partnership is kept up to speed and engaged?

If the business world, the Government and community groups are serious about wanting to work more in partnership, perhaps they ought to join together in setting up a 'School for Partnerships'. This would harness the expertise of organisations like Community Links and particular business partners, and offer modules on courses run by existing groups like Common Purpose, the Civil Service Top Management Programme and the various business schools – as well as offer its own courses.

Just imagine if, over the next two to three years, we could train up several thousand rising-star civil servants, business people and community entrepreneurs – then the ambition which many of us have had for a long time now to clone Community Links could be realised.

David Grayson CBE is a director of Business in the Community and chairman of the National Disability Council. He was chairman of Taskforce 2002 and was co-founder, in 1980, of Project North East

Cartoon by Steve Bell

'I've seen a photo of a street of terraced houses, and instead of a tarmac road with cars parked down both sides, the road is covered with grass. Some boys were playing football on it. I thought to myself, I want to live on a street like that'

Mavis, 39

Number 15
Newham: an A–Z

WILLIAM BOYD

Spotted Dogs, strange hieroglyphics, dry-ski slopes and Zoroastrians... A walk through the streets of Newham throws up the most unexpected details

Aeroplanes announce Newham to the approaching traveller as they steeply climb and bank above this distant and forgotten borough of London. The STOL-jets and prop-planes from the City Airport strain skyward. Nobody looks up: people pay as much attention to these soaring aircraft as they would to a dog barking.

Barking Road, Newham's old commercial spine, was built early in the 19th century to connect the East and West India docks with the river port of Barking. Now it wears the familiar garb of every urban high street: franchise chains and letting agencies, car sale-rooms, pubs and shuttered shops. Here and there the odd 1960s high-rise. Rows of two-storey terraced houses lead off on either side. The Boer War lingers here in pockets – Mafeking Road, Kimberley Road – and little bits of Scotland – Glasgow Road, Tweedmouth Road, Perth Road. Bright doors speak of stubborn house pride: cerise, mauve, moss green, canary.

Canary Wharf's solid blunt obelisk looms everywhere, over house gables, dominating the western horizon, confronting you as you turn corners. Margaret Thatcher's real lasting monument, a concrete and glass hymn to commerce, capitalism and market forces rising heftily, beefily, out of the Isle of Dogs.

Dogs shit freely on Newham's streets as they do throughout London, in Chelsea and Mayfair as well as in Barnet and Peckham. And dogs run free around the estates behind the Barking Road. The few dogs on leashes look at their free-ranging brothers enviously, longing to be released.

William Boyd Newham: an A–Z

East London goes on forever, the great 'other city' within the vast spreading mass of London. Cut off from the west by the office towers of the Square Mile, it runs from Stepney to Dagenham, onwards and onwards. The sluggish flow of traffic on the arterial roads glints in the afternoon sun like the scales of fish.

Fish still swim in Roding Creek, I suppose. One hundred and fifty years ago Barking was a fishing port with over two hundred Barking smacks and a thousand men and boys to man them. Now the northern outfall of London's main drainage decants here at the mouth of Roding Creek where it joins the Thames. The air is rank with the smell of gas.

Gasworks can provide a kind of immortality. Beckton Gasworks are so called after Simon Adams Beck, governor of the Gas Light and Coke Co., who bought the site at East Ham in 1867. Beck-town grew and grew and became the largest gasworks in the world. On the map all colours cease at Beckton: it remains white, the gasometers, the tanks and the filter-beds marked as neat rows of circles – strange hieroglyphics.

Hieroglyphics badge Newham's walls today, the graffiti and the tags of the urban young, a form of writing that can be found replicated in Paris, Rio and Manhattan. Tribal markings that defy the local – all seemingly written in the same crazed hand – which are, bizarrely, truly international.

'International cheap phonecalls' proclaims the sign above a shop window, an audacious oxymoron. Indeed, 'international' appears to be a favoured adjective in Newham. 'International hair styling', says another shop window. There is 'International rowing', also, at the regatta centre, and you can pray for your misbegotten soul at

15

the Amazing Grace International Worship Centre on Barking Road. Two senses of 'international' operate here: one is about inclusion – come one, come all – one is about keeping up with the Joneses.

Jones Scrap Metal, at the beginning of Barking Road, is reputedly the biggest in London, which is a not-to-be-sneezed-at claim-to-fame for Canning Town. Another feather in Newham's cap is the City Airport. Amongst London boroughs only Hounslow can boast a fully-fledged international airport (that word again). You can fly all over Europe from Newham, to Rotterdam and Amsterdam, Paris and Brussels – which is not bad from a borough generally regarded to be on the skids.

Kids mooch around in tatty recreational areas, kids with bikes and skateboards, all colours, all nationalities. The walls and the sheds and garage roofs around them are all crowned with barbed-wire or razor wire or more complicated revolving impediments. Keep kids out, these hostile barriers seem to say, indications of deeper suspicions, no innocence here, a want of love.

Lovage Approach is the new Newham, south of Tollgate Road. Dinky, villagey lanes, with small, clustered brick houses, leaded diamond-paned glass in the windows, porches and dormer-windows, a hotch-potch of domestic styles. Architects creating a 'community', here reaching back to their notional roots – reckless pillaging from a catalogue of olde-worlde vernacular styles – as we start the new Millennium.

Millennium Mills still stands, built decades before the Millennium Dome, not so far away. A monument to the borough's industrial past when the 'offensive trades' were ordered out of metropolitan London and were obliged to set up shop in the east along the

Thames. An industrial base almost vanished now, impossible to rebuild or renew.

New City Road turns off Barking Road. A long run of terraced houses. On either side are other identical streets, Kingsland Road, Patrick Road... Avenues of neatly pollarded plane trees, houses built in the 19th century for clerks working in the City. This could be Fulham or Battersea 20 years ago. Now with the new 'villages' proliferating perhaps this is all there is in Newham that is really old.

'Old' Newham never really existed, however. The borough was created in 1965 – the county boroughs of East Ham and West Ham brought together with bits of Plaistow and Woolwich and Upton. 'Ham' means low-lying pasture.

Pasture is hard to find today. There are angular bits of waste ground, thick with buddleia and rose-bay willow-herb, abandoned tracts of land between spur roads and the wire-mesh walls of tyre depots and scrap-metal merchants. Strangely, along the Royal Albert Dock Spine Road there is a sudden profusion of allotments, well tended. Things are growing here: runner-beans and potatoes, lettuce and cabbages. Prince Albert would be pleased, I think, to see such husbandry and enterprise, and so would his Queen.

Queen Victoria's presence still leaves a marked trace. All the royal docks are in the borough. Her own Victoria Dock, her husband's Albert Dock, and her grandson's dock, George V. The City Airport sits between Albert and George like an aircraft-carrier moored in a wide placid river.

River views are distant ones in Newham. The docks dominate the river here: huge wind-flurried rectangles of water reflecting the

15

turbulent skyscape. And the sewage jetties and the sludge piers of Beckton hog the river bank at Gallions Reach as the Thames's northern meander turns east again. From a spine road you can catch a glimpse of the scalloped towers of the Thames Flood Barrier, shining like burnished steel.

Steel shutters on modest shops – newsagents, electrical goods – tell you something about a place. Many shops selling second-hand furniture tell you something about a place. But just when you think you have Newham sited in its demographic circle of hell you see the dry-ski run – the Beckton Alps Ski Centre – and the Asda superstore. The contrasts abound: pie and mash for sale and McDonald's Drive-Thru; boarded-up, torched flats and bijou pseudo-villages. And everywhere streets bulging with traffic.

Traffic lights in Newham seem set longer than anywhere else in London. 'The borough doesn't like motorists,' a minicab driver confides. The wait seems to go on forever. And look at all the speed-bumps. Yet most people's view of the place is from a car – passing through, heading east or west, on a spine road or a flyover – or from the tall gantries of the Docklands Light Railway. Rare names appear which ring a distinct bell – West Ham, of course – and others that provoke fainter recognitions – Custom House, Silvertown (can there be a place in London called Silvertown?), Canning Town and Upton.

Upton Park, it is hard to believe, had – in the 18th century – a botanic garden second only to Kew, hence its name. It is famous now for being home to West Ham F.C., for some of the worst housing in Europe and for the Spotted Dog, the oldest pub in the borough, which dates from the 16th century. The Spotted Dog – *ave atque vale.*

'Valediction forbidding mourning.' Can there be a stranger borough in London? Can there be images of the city more dramatically bleak and excitingly futuristic? The wind seems keener and fiercer in Newham than elsewhere in London, tugging at you as it rushes from across the North Sea and the Thames estuary, hurrying on its giant flotilla of dark rain clouds, spinnakering westwards. Stand on the dockside at the City Airport and watch the planes lift off for Frankfurt and Bruges, your eye momentarily held by the flashing light at the tip of Canary Wharf, your ear catching the rumble of a train on the elevated trackways of the DLR – as you turn you note the precisely angled slope of the dry-ski run and the bright stacked apartments of a new village-cluster and, behind you, the fuming steel ziggurat that is the Tate & Lyle sugar factory. Some sort of weird rejuvenation is happening here out in the east of London, however surreal. The mineral rain spits on your face, abrading your cheeks gently, as with a fine steel-wool.

Woolwich, or to be more precise, North Woolwich, forms the southern most portion of the borough, and, because the rest of Woolwich was south of the river – in Kent – it was known, until it was amalgamated into Newham, as 'Kent in Essex'.

Xeroxing a map of Newham and noticing how it is composed of so many real places with real histories made me realise how artificial a construct it is. So I suggest we should abandon its current pronunciation, the apologetic half-swallowed mumble of 'newum', and boldly re-christen it New Ham, which, along with the ancient low-lying meadows of East and West Ham, might give the place a sense of continuity and a kind of validity – make it seem less young.

Young boroughs lack traditions, lack a sense of community.

Newham has existed for only 35 years. West Ham, by contrast, is an ancient parish and was even a parliamentary borough in 1855, and, moreover, one that played a significant role in the history of socialism. Keir Hardie was elected Labour MP for West Ham South in 1892. Neville Chamberlain suspended its Board of Guardians in 1926 for what the government regarded as over-generous poor relief. What can youthful Newham offer in terms of history and tradition that won't seem wholly *ersatz*?

Zoroastrianism may seem an unlikely notion, even a facetious one, but Newham and its agglomeration of parishes and county bor-oughs has always been a home to non-conformity and pluralism. There were over a hundred non-conformist chapels of all denom-inations at the turn of the century; there were Quaker meeting houses in Plaistow in the 17th century and the borough still boasts two convents and two friaries. I'm sure that today any passing Zoroastrian would receive a warm welcome in Amazing Grace's International Worship Centre on Barking Road. You look around at all the contrasts and contradictions of the place and have to conclude that, whatever its difficulties, its transformations and its deprivations, the real and enduring spice in Newham's life has always been its ineffable, unrivalled and bewildering variety.

William Boyd's latest novel is *Armadillo* (Penguin, £6.99)